out of the depths

"In *Out of the Depths,* Gebara presents a fresh, insightful reflection on the nature of evil and the experience of it that women—particularly marginalized women—face. She examines concrete examples and reconstructs the ideas of evil and salvation from a scholarly, feminist, and distinctly practical perspective. Ultimately, even in the face of the struggles and evil that Gebara documents in this book, she offers hope by way of her workable vision of a more balanced, ethical, life-giving world."

— *U.S. Catholic*

out of the depths
WOMEN'S EXPERIENCE OF EVIL AND SALVATION

Ivone Gebara

translated by Ann Patrick Ware

Fortress Press
Minneapolis

OUT OF THE DEPTHS
Women's Experience of Evil and Salvation
Translated from the French by Ann Patrick Ware

Cover art copyright © 2002 José Ortega/Images.com. Used by permission.
Cover design: Marti Naughton
Interior design: Beth Wright

Scripture quotations are from the New Revised Standard Version Bible, copyright © 1989 by the Division of Christian Education of the National Council of the Churches of Christ in the USA, and are used by permission.

Library of Congress Cataloging-in-Publication Data
Gebara, Ivone.
    [Mal au féminin. English]
    Out of the depths : women's experience of evil and salvation / Ivone Gebara ; translated by Ann Patrick Ware.
        p.   cm.
    Includes bibliographical references and index.
    ISBN 0-8006-3475-6 (pbk. : alk. paper)
        1. Feminist theology. 2. Woman (Philosophy) 3. Good and evil. I. Title.

BT83.55 .G4413 2002
230'.082—dc21

                                                            2002018965

The paper used in this publication meets the minimum requirements of American National Standard for Information Sciences — Permanence of Paper for Printed Library Materials, ANSI Z329.48-1984.

Manufactured in the U.S.A.   AF 1-3475
06   05   04   03   02   1   2   3   4   5   6   7   8   9   10

contents

translator's note

When I first received my copy of *Le mal au féminin*, I set about reading portions of it every day. As I got further and further into Ivone Gebara's thought, I kept wanting to share her ideas with friends. There was nothing to do but to set about translating, first, passages I found especially exciting, and then the whole book. Translating was for me a work of love and friendship.

A happy fortune had already put me in touch with Ivone Gebara. When she came to New York in 1994 to teach at Auburn Seminary, she wanted help polishing her English for the lectures she had prepared. Someone suggested my name. I had heard of Ivone as one of Latin America's leading feminist philosophers and theologians, and when we met, during the first moments of conversation, we made a great transnational leap. This was possible, of course, because of Ivone's amazing openness to new friendships, her warmth, her ready smile. In our working sessions, when syntax or vocabulary hindered my understanding of Ivone's thought, we had French as a common language. And we had gestures! And we had much laughter!

Ivone was already under the scrutiny of the Vatican for having favored the legalization of abortion in Brazil. She knew from association with her poor neighbors the cruel circumstances that drive some women to seek backstreet abortions and how those abortions often result in maternal deaths. Legalization, she said, was only one small aspect of a broader struggle in what she called "an abortive society," that is, a society that does not offer jobs, health care, housing, or education to poor women.

Vatican officials were outraged and put pressure on Ivone's religious congregation to control her thought and speech. Long discussions followed; and although Brazil's presiding bishop closed the case, other Vatican authorities began to review her positions on the image of God, the divinity of Jesus, and the patriarchal structure of the church. The result was that Ivone's religious congregation, at the insistence of the Vatican, levied the sanction of reeducation in "traditional theology." Ivone, already possessing a doctorate in philosophy and broad education in theology, was to go to school again in the heart of Catholic Europe and get it right this time. She therefore earned another doctorate, this time in Religious Sciences, from the Pontifical Catholic University of Louvain. Her degree was conferred, with highest honors, in the name of Pope John Paul II!

Ivone Gebara once described herself as a "naughty bee accused of producing a honey of a different flavor." Translating her thought is an exercise in ingenuity. Her honey, as she herself described it, comes from frequenting forbidden gardens and touching base with hitherto unrecognized sources. Produced in a different "nonscientific" manner, it is intoxicating and disconcerting. May you find it so!

Ann Patrick Ware

introduction

Evil has always been spoken of as an experience common to both women and men. No one who lives on any social or responsible level is exempt from it. No one, even the person without any personal experience of evil, can live outside the historic fabric of solidarity within the mystery of good and evil. The problem that captivates my thinking is not the existence of evil, but rather the understanding of it, the way it is interpreted, and especially the role this interpretation has played in history and theology, particularly in relationship to women. What I mean by *evil* will become clear as we go along, but I would like to explain a few points at the beginning.

Everyday Evil

The evil I want to talk about is not the evil we do personally, but the evil that we undergo, that we suffer or endure, something not chosen, the kind of evil present in institutions and social structures that accommodate it, even facilitate it. Evil of this sort has no connection with conscience or choice. It is sometimes beyond recognition. One lives with it daily; one sometimes endures it without even naming it as evil. Moreover, it often happens that this kind of evil is accepted as fate, as God's design or as punishment for hidden sins. Evil is so mixed in with our existence that we can live in it without even taking account of it as evil. I'm thinking particularly of those men and women who are executioners in dictatorships, soldiers fighting in war, and those who by their activity keep a system of violence and injustice operating. This "work" is their livelihood, but it also produces evil. I'm thinking also of countless women who live in almost blind obedience in their homes or in religious institutions, without taking any notice of the exploitation that they endure and that, in a certain sense, they copy.

We might ask when evil becomes evil. Do we have to be conscious of it to denounce it? Does someone have to name it and bring its noxious character into the limelight? By what criterion can we declare it evil? These questions give us an inkling that it is not simple to define evil's domain. Even if it is possible to speak objectively about evil or about fighting against evil, it is not simple to discern it personally, especially when it permeates a larger social structure.

Some deeds become evil through excess; some through insufficiency. Evil may result even when we have good intentions. If we are to denounce evil, we need a critical conscience to make its depravity evident. We need certain agreed-upon criteria to recognize its features as damaging to a person or a group. We need a certain prophetic quality. Philosophy and psychology can unveil the connections that produce violence or marginalization. This process is bound up with the dynamic of human history. We often observe a kind of shrouding of evil in our behaviors, making it difficult to grasp even if sometimes it seems apparent. Evil is the bad seed sown in the midst of the good, difficult to distinguish and root out. Evil is also like leaven mixed in the dough. Sometimes it began as something good and degenerated into evil. These comparisons make the distinction between good and evil even more obscure. Can we say, as we do in the case of leaven, that it seems to be and is always good? I think evil can be leaven too; paradoxically, it can cause the dough to rise.

Some kinds of evil are readily condemned. But in the case of events intermingled in our culture, education, and religion— events or behaviors regarded as normal, common, even good—it is not easy to spot evil's presence even when we suspect it is there. For example, we often have difficulty detecting evil in the privileged habitat of women, the domestic scene. I propose a feminist theology that addresses the evil present in the domestic milieu, that arena of relations between men and women, that place of private history, that unavowed sphere of hierarchy and exclusion.

Evil and Women

Speaking about evil as lived and performed by women is a complex business. When we turn our attention to experiences of destruction, alienation, or exclusion, which are the daily fare of women, conflicts arise about understanding and interpretation. Just as there is no real agreement in speaking about the evil suffered by men, so there is none about the evil undergone by women. Certainly, people will agree about the evil present in situations of physical and, especially, sexual violence. Nevertheless, a whole range of deeds deriving from cultural and religious customs appear as sinister only when viewed by a critical analysis outside of the typical understanding of human relations. Only specialists would be able to discover the destructive intentions of certain cleverly structured systems of thought.

The church, an institution created and dominated by men, has interpreted women's experience of evil, whether undergone or committed by women, in a way that bears little or no resemblance to what women feel or ask for, whether in theology or within the structures of the church. The same can be said for the means of salvation. These means are tightly bound to a male religious approach that presents itself as universalist; any differences are subsumed into global egalitarian speech, which often hides its particular character. All of this context once again renders the question of evil complex and makes its definition problematic. For this reason it is important to hear accounts of concrete experiences and to situate them in a culture and context, to look at the possible results and the specific hopes they contain.

A Male View of Evil

I am persuaded that, if we are to probe into the question of evil, we have to develop a new anthropology.[1] Without pursuing that here, I do propose some principles of anthropology that are different from those developed in Christian tradition and are bound to new hermeneutical tools. My reflection in no way negates the positive nature of tradition, but it does take note of its deficiency in the face of today's new cultural challenges.

Some rather complicated questions can be raised about the philosophical anthropology that supports Christian theology in general. For instance, when the question of evil arises, we discover throughout Christian tradition a male-defined view of reality as a hierarchy based on dualisms. More precisely, this means that evil, as far as men are concerned, has always been viewed as some "thing" that happens, that takes hold of human beings, surrounds them, attracts them. Furthermore, for men, evil is not inherent to human nature; rather, it results from freedom—limited freedom, of course, but free will all the same. In the case of women, however, certain Scripture texts and a number of theological commentaries by church fathers state that female beings are more evil than male beings. This interpretation has long prevailed in theology.

For men, evil is an act one can undo. But for women, evil is in their very being. To be female is from the start something bad or at least something limiting. And thus the evil women commit springs from their corrupt being, which is held more responsible for the fall, the disobedience of the human being toward God. Thus, at bottom this anthropological position reveals a conflict in our very understanding of what it means to be human. Traditional theology affirms man as good in the beginning, but it falls into the trap of Manichaeism, or dualistic thinking, when dealing with woman. It all but identifies woman with evil as if women incarnate evil. Similarly, man is considered primarily or normatively the image of God, while woman is only secondarily that image through her soul, quite independent of her femaleness. Marriage blessed by

God redeems woman through motherhood and integrates her into the couple, where she comes to share in the image of God.[2]

We must add that this position is largely based on an extremely limited interpretation of the myth in Genesis about the origins of the human race and evil. This interpretation is permeated with philosophical and religious hierarchical dualisms as well as the biblical editors' thinly veiled political bias.[3]

Before the advent of historical critique and text redaction, Scripture commentators often read passages literally and taught them as being indicative of God's will. This interpretation, in spite of the evolution in biblical studies, is still present in our religious culture and is used as the basic myth supporting prejudice against women. The myth is accepted not only by religious institutions but even by common discourse as representing the role of woman: she is seductress and at the same time under man's control. In various cities of Latin America, the symbol of an apple with a bite taken out designates places of prostitution or sites for illicit trysts, where the seductive power of women renews the sin of human origins.

The fact that a reader can discern in biblical texts a difference in nature between man and woman reveals how early culture was influenced by seeing women as second-class beings. This view of women stretches back into history at least as far as biblical texts, with their emphasis on the difference between the sexes. The hierarchical dualism that serves as foundation for a kingdom of lords and slaves is the same lens used in certain Scriptures to favor the exclusion of women. Still, we must remember that this exclusion, especially in the church, has undergone variations in the course of history; in the Middle Ages, for example, there was a certain expansion of thought about women and sexuality.[4] But this was a discrepancy and not the norm.

Feminist readings of the Bible introduce a suspicion, not only as to its original composition or redaction of texts, but especially to its interpretation through the ages. For example, let us look at 1 Tim. 2:9-15, which was widely used in the teachings of the church of yesterday and is still invoked by the contemporary church, even though today's language is a bit different. This passage is surely dependent on the culture of the time and merely reproduces then-current conduct. Nevertheless, it is important to recall it inasmuch as the whole Bible is affirmed as the "Word of God."

> . . . The women should dress themselves modestly and decently in suitable clothing, not with their hair braided, or with gold, pearls, or expensive clothes, but with good works, as is proper for women who profess reverence for God. Let a woman learn in silence with full submission. I permit no woman to teach or to have authority over a man; she is to keep silent. For Adam was formed first, then Eve; and Adam was not deceived, but the woman was deceived and became a transgressor. Yet she will be saved through childbearing, provided they continue in faith and love and holiness, with modesty. (1 Tim. 2:9-15)

Questions and suspicions occur to me as I read these instructions. Why insist so much on the submission of women? Why insist that it was Eve who allowed herself to be tricked? And why limit salvation for women to childbearing—submissive, chaste, and holy? What is proposed for men? What marks out their path of salvation? Men have always marked out their own path even if they say they are obeying God. Why do women need a twofold mediation to be saved—that of God and that of men—while men need only one? Whose salvation matters anyway?

I am not interested in accusing or taking a stand against the past. Rather, I am attempting to overcome in the present the past injustices we now see and to create more respectful relationships between women and men. A feminist reading of the Bible proposes hypotheses that lead us to think critically, to ask the reason for the author's admonitions and wonder whether he was afraid of women's leadership in the Christian community. Suspicion becomes a working tool in feminist research.

Silence about Evil

Discourse about evil as well as its definition has always given preference to evil as men perceive it, with no reference to the evil actually borne by women. Evil as women know it has been reduced to silence. It is almost unknown; where it is known, from men's perspective, it is almost the worst of all evils, belonging to the very essence of woman. Frequently, what men perceive is woman herself as evil: their view demonizes woman. We need only to consult the mass of works in the Western tradition that speak of women as witches or purveyors of wickedness. For example, Jean Delumeau, in his work on the history of fear in Western culture, gives us valuable information on the historical fear of women and the conviction that women were agents of the devil.[5]

But there is no information about the way women themselves lived or the accusations against them. Women's words are nowhere to be found: women are silent victims even when they succeed in gaining a mention in official history. Moving from silence to public speech is the purpose of this study. The voices of women will remind various institutions, including the churches, of the urgency of establishing respect and equality between the sexes.

Just as the evil women endure is hidden, so too their sacrifices are ignored and regarded as worthless. We know that the hard things men endure, especially their sufferings, can be redemptive, but the evil women endure (suffering, self-sacrifice in favor of another) too often counts for nothing. We need only to remember that in Christianity the aspect of sacrifice that is salvific is basically male. Male sacrifice is the only kind that redeems and restores life; male blood is the only blood of any value. And this has been the case from the Old Testament to the New, right up to contemporary theologies. Women's bleeding is filthy, impure, dangerous. And it continues to be so in the Christian tradition, even though Jesus' experience with the hemorrhaging woman (Mark 5:21-43) shows otherwise. By addressing this contradictory view of sacrifice in our culture, I add my voice to those of many other women, whose lives act as witness.

My analysis is not particularly biblical, although I do make reference to Scripture from time to time. I prefer to work from the perspective of a theological anthropology, which I see as essential if we are to establish relationships of justice and solidarity. Such an anthropology may eventually be able to open doors leading to an end to the decree of the "curse of women" in our culture and in our theology. The "scandalous" voice of women, or the scandal of their words, will be able to be heard as a voice of salvation, a redemptive event, an attempt to restore justice within a structure of violence. The patriarchal and hierarchical understanding of Christianity, so rife in the tradition, will be opened to a nonpatriarchal perception, more open and democratic, with the limits that entails. Within these limits and in spite of the difficulty of equalizing rights between the sexes, there lies the problem of human sexuality. As Jean-Marie Aubert says, "Sexuality as a human and cultural phenomenon is probably the domain where ancient collective representations and old reactions remain at their most powerful, serving the need to dominate in order to make oneself more important."[6] Because the feminist battle is still only taking its first steps within the Catholic church, the church remains, as Aubert says, one of the last bastions of male domination.

Feminism in Latin America

My analysis, beyond the limits of conventional theological discourse, is based in contextual theology, which includes several elements of liberation theology. But these elements are reexamined in light of questions raised by women. In this sense, contextual theology takes seriously the lives and actions of the various agents in a culture, whether men or women. Further, to speak of evil undergone by women means opening consideration to cultural and sexual differences, with all their contradictions and riches.

This work is a feminist reflection; the shades of my feminist perspective will appear throughout this book. Nevertheless, it seems important to me to outline broadly the feminism I embrace.

The feminist movement in Latin America began to gain public recognition in the 1960s. The movement attracted a certain intellectual elite and some militants of the political left and has since developed vigorously as a social movement to gain women's rights at all levels of society. In contrast, the Latin American worlds of theology and the Catholic church have not been directly concerned with the question of women's rights. People thought that these issues belonged to women of the "first world," who were caught up in a bourgeois equality, lacking any political international dimension and alien to any preferential option for the poor. Concern about women's rights and attention to problems specific to women emerged only recently in the lives of Latin American Christian communities. Latin American feminism has two characteristics. The first is more popular and takes into consideration the practical cares of the daily life of poor women. The second is more academic and is devoted to rethinking the human sciences from a feminist perspective. Several Latin American universities now want to integrate a Center of Feminist Studies into their various departments. Academic publications and meetings are incorporating a feminist lens into their studies and debates.

My own feminism began developing early in the 1980s after reading books and articles by North American and German theologians, such as Rosemary Radford Ruether and Dorothee Soelle.[7] They refined my perception and made me more attentive to the expression, silence, and anguish of the women of Brazil. They provided tools to analyze behavior between men and women; they made me pay more attention to the power of the language generally accepted by society that makes the male normative; and they helped me to be more sensitive to contradictions in language about God.

I have never been a militant feminist; my feminism is primarily concerned with theology. Soon I began to think about concrete questions asked by laywomen, Sisters, and students about their reality as women in the face of certain theological formulations. I was not affiliated with any feminist group in North America or

Europe. Feminist theologians on these continents were concerned about academic classifications, a stance that I found limiting and even contradictory to their thought. Thus they spoke of radical feminists (like Mary Daly), critical feminists (like Elisabeth Schüssler Fiorenza, Rosemary Radford Ruether, Catherine Halkes), and moderate Christian feminists (like Letty Russell and Phyllis Trible).[8] I read many of their works, but I thought of myself as an independent intellectual feminist.

In fact, I was aware of the social, cultural, and religious oppression of women, and my feminist thought has developed from precise questions raised in the Latin American context. I recognize the importance of feminism, in spite of all its contradictions, as a social and political movement aiming toward relationships of equality and justice between men and women. I recognize too the importance of its analyses and hermeneutical tools used to uncover the systemic domination of one sex over the other. For several years now I have also been asking ecological questions, integrating concern for the safeguarding of the planet into my feminist analysis.

Gender

We know that feminism has forged new concepts in the last twenty years to analyze the condition of women.[9] Feminist theory speaks of *sexism* as discrimination toward the female sex, *phallocracy* or *androcracy* as affirming the centrality of male power, and *patriarchy*[10] to indicate a system perpetuated by the domination of men over women. The male figure represented by the father becomes the archetypal principle underlying the organization and understanding of the world. The concept of gender emerges as one of the most recent hermeneutical concepts introduced by Western feminism. Gender was introduced by American feminists in the 1980s and taken up shortly thereafter by French and Quebec feminists.[11]

The category of gender includes two interconnected dimensions. The first acknowledges that the biological reality of the human being is not enough to explain the behavioral differences of male and female in society; the concept of gender encompasses more than biological sex. Gender is a "socially learned concept, manifested, institutionalized, and transmitted from generation to generation."[12] Thus, in certain aspects, a person becomes a man or a woman according to certain cultural and social expectations. The second dimension of gender is tied to the notion of power. We observe that power is distributed unequally between the sexes; women hold subordinate positions in society and also in organized Western religions. The two fundamental qualities of gender affect relationships between women and men not only in the home but also in the broader social arena.

From the point of view of the social sciences, introducing the concept of gender has modified hitherto cherished theories and ideologies. Gender has also slowly begun to be used by theologians, especially women, and in particular North American women. In this work I use the concept of gender to analyze the problem of evil, employing literature, testimonial evidence, and certain contemporary theological interpretations. This new interpretive tool opens creative ways to further the understanding of the complexity of evil in human existence.

My phenomenological analyses are limited to certain literary texts that convey women's experience of evil. I have no intention of creating a phenomenological theory of literature or a treatise on phenomenological philosophy;[13] rather, I will use the insights of the phenomenological method, particularly in its ability to describe the reality of daily life and the spoken word in order to apprehend present meaning. I acknowledge the influence of the phenomenology and hermeneutic of Paul Ricoeur, notably in his work *Philosophy of the Will*.[14] His methods of listening to disclosures of sins and confessions of faith and examining the universe of myths are the inspiration for my own approach.

The texts I have chosen give preference to the Latin American experience, but not in any absolute way. I had to look outside my culture for the expression of some of my own intuitions and for certain aspects of evil endured and expressed by women of other cultures and religions. I describe some of my own experience of evil so as to be faithful to the path proposed by feminism and lived by a good number of women in Latin America and elsewhere. What strikes me are the similarities among quite different experiences. The universal experience of distress and grief leads us to take note of a certain "geography of evil," which characterizes the life of women, especially poor women, everywhere. Moreover, an appeal to God or to a transcendent mystery occurs everywhere in these accounts of daily afflictions. This is what we find in all the testimonies even though they derive from different cultures and ages.

Developing a new way of thinking about what it means to be human seems to be a challenge absolutely essential for our times. And to think about evil from a woman's perspective forms part of this challenge: we must build more equitable relations and a greater solidarity in the Christian world and beyond. This is the hope and goal of this book.

CHAPTER 1

women's experience of evil

By examining women's experience of evil, by listening to women about what makes their experience different, we can come to understand the specificity of evil as women live it. At the very heart of women's experience of suffering we may discover the meaning of evil and try to understand its power. But in attempting to do so, we need to listen to voices with many tonalities, to take account of particular nuances in their cries, to note the difference in their plaints and their sufferings. We need to identify new places, those not yet sufficiently recognized, where evil flourishes.

My work takes its direction from words about particular lives, that is, women's lives; my approach is based on a feminist phenomenology, an attempt to explore women's experiences, especially the harmful ones. In analyzing women's experience of evil, I do not intend to develop a systematic theory of phenomenology as Edmund Husserl, Paul Ricoeur, and others have done, but I have drawn freely from their insights in exploring the testimony of the witnesses cited in this chapter. Here in this book I employ the words women use to describe the suffering of their daily lives.

A Feminist Phenomenology

Phenomenology is one way to approach reality. It reveals the mundane existence of most people, not only as it actually is but also as we interpret it. It opens the way for different perspectives and starting points for dealing with the same subject. That is why this method is suited to a feminist approach to the subject of evil. A phenomenology must rely on the data of concrete existence, on things that appear in the field of our experience.[1] Interpretation and later reflection use this experience. Phenomenology does not explain outside events but tries to understand them from within, even though it may never lead to having clear and distinct ideas. The phenomenology of women's evil is an epistemological attempt to grasp and understand the specifics of evil for women. It introduces new elements. We need to be influenced by the testimonies of women and to enter into the interpretations they make of them. These interpretations, especially those in writing, are not numerous, but I consider it essential to present in this chapter some of those that are available.

The experience of evil appears under many expressions. For this reason trying to understand this multiplicity must accommodate a broad complexity. Evil is *evils,* not one thing, but many—the sufferings people undergo according to their condition, their locale, and also their biological and cultural situation. To speak of difference may seem to be an intellectual distinction not observable in daily life. Promoting the ideal of the universal equality of human beings often hides actual inequality in our history and culture.

This hiddenness affects many more women than men, more blacks than whites, more poor than rich. Generalizations are easily come by and frequently used but may distort reality. So we have to ask: What does evil experienced by women mean? What women are we talking about? Where is this particular kind of evil likely to appear?

In answering these questions I give preference to a certain type of testimony highlighting the experience of poor and oppressed women, those who, by force of habit, are more silent than others. I want to reflect on the concrete evils of women caught in social and cultural structures that put them in an inferior position in the hierarchy of human beings. This means that I concentrate on specific evils suffered by women and not on the broad universal female experience. Moreover, to speak of evil for women introduces the concept of gender at the outset. Even though I deal more systematically with that concept in a later chapter, I need to make note of it here as an interpretive tool.

This notion of gender enables us to grasp the difference between men's and women's experience of evil even when other important elements are present. It also uncovers the "regional" character of this experience, although some common factors allow us to speak of the human lot of evil and suffering. The universal is indeed found in personal experiences of evil, but we need to understand the specifics to be able to give meaning to what we call *universal*. Understanding the particular will reveal more clearly the ambiguity and complexity of the problem. Such reflection leads us to the question of personal and collective responsibility in the doing of evil. As Hannah Arendt writes,

> . . . Every generation, by virtue of being born into a historical continuum, is burdened by the sins of the fathers as it is blessed with the deeds of the ancestors. But this kind of responsibility is not what we are talking about here; it is not personal, and only in a metaphorical sense can one say he *feels* guilty for what not he but his father or his people have done. (Morally speaking, it is hardly less wrong to feel guilty without having done something specific than it is to feel free of all guilt if one is actually guilty of something.)[2]

Both phenomenology and the concept of gender will help us to take special note of women's responsibility in the execution of different forms of evil. We want to go beyond those simplistic and dualistic forms that claim to find a clear distinction between the guilty and the innocent.

The preferred way of expressing the evil women have experienced is to have women themselves tell about their experiences; sometimes those who have witnessed it, including men, may be able to tell the story. Some men are, in fact, by their sensitivity, proximity, and support of women able to express what women go through. They are able, by reason of their humanity, to feel moved by a tragedy of which thousands of women are victims. They are able to feel what crushes the body of another, even if their own bodies are biologically and culturally different. Clearly the quality of the witness is important if the testimony is to be true and compelling. Giving witness reveals the commitment, the life choices, the sensitivity, and the values of those who choose to give it.

Through certain passages tied to daily experience, I would like, first of all, to try to capture the evil experienced by women. This method, though full of ambiguity, may begin to unravel the problem that engrosses us. Women's acknowledgment of their difficult condition can help us reach the place where their rescue may occur. The place of evil, of unhappiness, of often incomprehensible suffering carries within it a call to salvation or some provisional path to freedom. I believe such to be the case even if this path consists of merely condemning the actual suffering.

The texts gathered in this chapter relate sufferings considered evil directly or indirectly. Before we try to understand in any systematic sense the meaning of their evilness, we must listen to the women describe them. And as we read the texts, a first interpretation will unfold from within their narration. To relate is already to interpret. To read the narration is already to reinterpret what has been related. This constitutes the first step of a phenomenological approach to evil. It is phenomenology at work, that is, the presence of the subject who gives an interpretation by telling the facts of her existence. It is also the presence of the other one, the one who listens or who reads and tries to understand. To understand is also to interpret.

We are dealing here with narrating evil that is present and simultaneously evil from the past. Once suffering is described, even if it is going on at the time, it contains something of the past at the very moment it is being mentioned. The wound as it is being spoken of already exists at a certain distance from the event. It is there as a narrated memory, and as such it contains an interpretation. The exact moment of the sorrow is not grasped, but what is grasped is the moment told, understood, interpreted in light of the present. Even if the experience of evil is always present, the act of relating the story means to be not entirely caught in the suffering that the moment produced.

The distance between women's telling about their experience of evil and the experience itself is not only indispensable but revealing of our human condition. We are beings who are always telling stories, and every time we do, we preserve traces of the past and the light of the present. The present changes our understanding of the past and of ourselves. The present introduces new means whereby we can understand the past, sometimes enlarging and sometimes narrowing its meaning.

The Power of Witnessing

The phenomenology of evil as women see it, whether in literature, song, art, or other forms of expression, is a work of memory past and present revealing the continuous existence of suffering. Through memory speech is freed; the dead are permitted to speak, and anguish can be relived in order to denounce whatever it is that keeps us from living with dignity.[3]

The books and voices I am using focus on Latin America, but not exclusively. Texts outside our own culture are quite capable of giving an accurate picture of misery despite a different setting. I have no single criterion for selecting material. I have looked in the writings of women for their experiences of evil in situations related to ownership, power, value, and skin color. These areas are intrinsic to human living and can thus help our reflection. Doubtless other important passages exist, but I have chosen these as a sample. I begin with a woman's experience in India, recounted in a novel by Kamala Markandaya; it illustrates several elements common in the lives of poor women throughout the world.

Women's Lack of Ownership

It is well known that in all societies the primary responsibility of feeding the family falls to women. Beginning with the nourishing function of the female body, lactation, culture imposes heavy responsibility upon women—the responsibility of feeding and educating their children and inculcating virtue—but it also oppresses, manipulates, and even destroys them. Women suffer in a special way when there is no food or drink for children. It is women who are accused of not feeding their family suitably. They are the ones who have to find ways to obtain food when there is none. Woman's life seems to be tied to the primary aspect of maintaining life. Consequently the evil of lacking the essentials of life touches them in a special way.

This fact is brought home to us in *Nectar in a Sieve,* a striking novel by the Indian writer Kamala Markandaya.[4] Even from within her particular cultural context she portrays a native female poverty as having universal elements, including both suffering and evil. But this "universal" is neither immutable nor definitive. It is a cultural, social universal, that is, a historic construction, and therefore changeable.

Markandaya describes the poignant story of a poor family in India. We accompany Ruku step by step. She is a woman full of life's dreams, a woman shaped by the lack of means of existence, a woman who sees her dreams crumble one by one because of poverty and the exploitation of the poor. Her destiny, marked by an ever-present hope, allows us to accompany these poor women on the path to search for dignity and recognition.

> At last no option but to draw upon my secret hoard: a small stock of rice, ten ollocks in all, shielded from every temptation to sell or barter, kept even when the need to hold our land had squeezed us dry of everything else. Now I brought it out and measured it again, ten ollocks exactly. Then I divided it into several equal portions, each of the portions as little as would suffice for one day.[5]

We may wonder whether the daily search for food is really an evil because it shows us the tenacity of Ruku, her persistence in seeking to keep her family alive. But even more than the social injustice of this situation and the presence of social evil, a heavy burden of expectation is laid on women to be the ones to provide food. In many cases, this cultural responsibility becomes an evil that hinders the development of women's lives. In general, men work to bring home money, but to plan the food—to divide it up, to see to it that it benefits the whole family—is a responsibility and a worry only for women.

Similarly, it is commonplace to leave to women the care of the sick and the dead because they are expected to be the main witnesses to life and death. Rubbing shoulders with the extremes of life is their assigned role. And since their bodies give life in the midst of pain and joy, culture seems to have fashioned them to welcome proximity to sickness and death. Women are often the ones to receive into their arms the wounded from war, suffering children, and dying old men.

Ruku's words over her dead son make us tremble: "For this I have given you birth, my son, that you should lie in the end at my feet with ashes in your face and coldness in your limbs and yourself departed without trace, leaving this huddle of bones and flesh without meaning."[6] The suffering of women in the face of children's sickness or death, especially in the midst of material poverty, is their special experience of evil. It is as though a part of themselves is torn away, abandoned, dead. And this loss is often accompanied by a feeling of guilt, which sometimes they are able to reject, but often in their conformity to culture they feel they deserve.

Markandaya continues to take us skillfully along Ruku's path. After the long harsh march of survival, a journey full of surprises and difficulties of every kind, she receives the suffering body of her husband, Nathan, breathing his last.

> They laid my husband on the paved floor and I sank down beside him. Somebody brought a light, a hurricane lantern that burned steady in the stormy wind; someone else, water. His body was caked in mud, wet and dirty. I wiped him clean, took his head in my lap. . . .
>
> And so I laid my face on his and for a while his breath fell soft and light as a rose petal on my cheek, then he sighed as if

in weariness and turned his face to me, and so his gentle spirit withdrew and the light went out in his eyes.[7]

We need to remember that it is culture that imposes the burden of caring for the sick and dying as a particular responsibility for women and implies that it belongs to them by nature. Evil is not the work women do but something imposed upon them or determined to be their proper role.

The body, that unique site of suffering and joy, always witnesses one's daily life; the very body that brings forth life also engenders pleasure and sometimes pleasure sold to others for the sake of survival. Pleasure, a human experience full of ambiguity, can become as part of sexual activity a means of survival as well as the expression of life's delight and relationship with the ones we love. To sell sex in order to live and keep others alive is a trade known to women of every age. It is a place of crucifixion and oppression, especially when no other choice is possible.

I deliberately say "to sell sex" and not "to sell oneself" because the majority of women succeed in maintaining, in some fragile way, a private invisible space, a secret inviolable harbor for their desire for happiness. Some women are able to safeguard their personal integrity even when the situation pushes them to choices that do not correspond with their deepest inclinations. A woman's criterion is always to save her own life or to save the lives of those who depend on her.

Ruku notices that Ira, her daughter, offers her body (sex) in secret for money in order to save the life of her little brother dying of hunger: "I saw her go out in the dusk, sari tightly wrapped about her. Saw her walk to the town, along the narrow lane which ran past the tannery, following it to where it broadened with beedi shops along one side and tawdry stalls on the other, where men with bold eyes lounged smoking or drinking from frothing toddy pots."[8]

Markandaya describes these moving events in the life of Ruku with a sad poignant beauty. A mournful poetry rises from the innermost being of the writer as if to capture what is hidden behind the horror of the violence she describes. A kind of force moves us, touches us, and obliges us to go beyond the limits life imposes on us. Something profoundly human, delicately balanced between sobbing and tears, reveals the hidden beauty of the life in which one is destroyed and in which one destroys oneself. But one must have the eyes of an artist to see this beauty. Often the eyes of the sufferers are incapable of discovering the tragic beauty hidden behind their dreams of love or nourishment.

Sometimes pressures to protect life arise from what we regard as least important in the matter of oppression. It is as if something beyond oneself, some kind of fragile strength, a small hope, a spark allows movement forward. Nonconformity in the face of imposed suffering, a kind of resistance seems willing to face involuntary unhappiness. This seems to be the unconquerable cry of life, ever ready to make itself heard, persevering like a gentle breeze or an almost silent groan when the fear of suffering and death takes form in our flesh. All this is present in the behavior of Ruku and of so many other women whose stories are the nameless stories of daily resistance.

In these passages from *Nectar in a Sieve,* the author retells the experiences of evil as a witness rather than a direct sufferer. She hides herself behind her characters and sets before us life as prophetic word against evil, life as a work of art witnessing against injustices, suffering as a poetic cry in view of salvation. She uses her voice and her art to show how each person's story has tangled connections to the stories of many others. Indeed, while the story-telling expresses a limited segment of experience, it always returns us to other experiences. In this way it keeps a collective character while being the work of one person and one word limited to a single context. The art of storytelling reveals a practical wisdom that allows the reader to become gripped by the narrative, to take a stand before events, and to perceive the ethical distance between what is and what ought to be, or, in other words, between what is and the longed-for ideal.[9]

Women's Lack of Power

In works by Latin American authors, a message about suffering and evil, beginning with the experience of being a woman, joins many other lived experiences in different parts of the world. This is not a question of combining all the suffering of women but of showing something similar just in the fact of being female. We must not overlook the suffering derived from racial difference, class distinction, and other factors. But there are similarities between the poverty of women in India and that of women in the shantytowns of Rio de Janeiro and other cities in Brazil and Latin America.

Let me quote here a woman from Rio de Janeiro, Beti, who lives in one of the most violent ghettos of the region.

> Women of the shantytowns all suffer the same problems. They wash clothes. When there is water, there is no soap. When there is soap, there is no water. They carry a huge basket of laundry to go wash it in a stream. They go to work. They often have children to take care of. The husband gets home in a bad mood. He drinks, and the bad situation makes him drink. The wife argues with him. She often does not realize that it is society that causes these times of exhaustion, aggressiveness, upheaval. They have to get up at night because the rain is coming in the house. They can hear rats in the kitchen. They have to go take care of their little boy who has cut his foot while running after his ball in the street.[10]

This is the daily domestic reality of evil lived by the poor and especially by women. It is the hidden evil, the evil without fanfare, the evil that never enters into the annals of a country. The dailiness of this good/evil accompanies life's most vital physical needs. This is the location of destruction: the body consumed by hunger, the body dying of thirst, the body homeless, the body wasted by sickness, the body beaten, the body undergoing violence, the body lacking salvation. But there is a concrete salvation, an everyday salvation, a salvation of the here and now, a salvation for this life and this moment. It is a far cry from the grand projects of world economy, official statistics, a religious apocalypse, a far cry from the salvation of heaven and messianic promises.

This same monotony of evil is revealed in the life of Carolina Maria de Jesus, who, while living in the slums of São Paulo, succeeded for years in keeping a journal in which she recorded her daily activities, including collecting papers, boxes, and iron scraps from the streets to keep her children fed. Her diary, *Child of the Dark,* was published in Brazil and elsewhere.[11] It describes not only life in the slums but also the daily desperation endured by a black woman looking to preserve her dignity. It contains her hope in the midst of daily destitution and filth—hope of escape, of having adequate food for her children and herself, of enjoying life. Her journal is witness to her search for happiness.

> Today I am lucky. There were many papers in the street. . . .
>
> I got out of bed at four a.m. and went to carry water, then went to wash clothes. I didn't make lunch. There is no rice. . . . In the old days I sang. Now I've stopped singing, because the happiness has given way to a sadness that ages the heart. . . .
>
> I got out of bed at four a.m. to write. I opened the door and gazed at the starry sky. . . .
>
> Today I fixed rice and beans and fried eggs. What happiness. . . .[12]

Here is evil brought about by the fact of being female and poor. Carolina is black besides. She bears an additional evil, that of skin color. Concentrated in her single person are three experiences of evil, three "sins" that society assigns to her and that weigh her down. If there is a kind of cultural and social destiny in this situation, at the same time resistance reveals the weakness of destiny. It is the resistance of women who are poor, but also of women who are not so poor, who stand in solidarity, and who want to change unjust relationships. When women suffering the evil of dispossession and powerlessness fight for their dignity, they fight also for power over their lives. The evil of being female and poor in a society shaped by hierarchical, white, male forces can be detected in the innermost privacy of daily life.

The author Isabel Allende, in her book *Paula*, has also described a different experience of suffering, of evil in women's daily lives.[13] Her daughter Paula was in a coma for six months; she is the inspiration and principal theme of the book. The book was written partly in the hospital, partly in the trips to and from, as a way of escaping despair in the face of certain death. Allende writes, "Listen, Paula. I am going to tell you a story, so that when you wake up, you will not feel so lost."[14]

Addressing her daughter, Allende tells her own story, the story of her family, and the story of her country, Chile, especially during the period of the military dictatorship. She ties the events of her story to a broader background: family, nation, loves, and memories are all intermingled in the present sorrow. Grief evokes them and makes them live again in memory. Just to write about them seems to be a "plank" of salvation. Her way of telling about herself reveals how significantly her experience of evil is mixed in with the rest of her life, and, even though her experience is similar to that of some men, it is marked by the absolutely determinative factor of being female. This factor reveals the originality of her life and her reactions as she faces her life story.

What a struggle to find herself in a society in which men always have the last word! What a struggle to bring about good in a society ruled by a bloody dictatorship that upholds the well-being of a tiny privileged minority! The evil here is not something metaphysical or abstract, but a specific evil endured—no food, no freedom of expression, no equal access, no democracy. Hers is a country and a continent inhabited by evil. And this lived evil, narrated later, is combined with the evil of dying, the serene tragic waning away of her daughter's life.

Is that evil more relentless than the evil of the military dictatorship? Is it different? Indeed it is, but it is not the difference that makes the passion distinctive. More striking is the powerful resistance in both cases—a desire to restore the strength of life. It is essential not to let go, not to let this consuming evil have the last word.

Struggling against these two evils, different as they are, brings Allende to a new point in her life. In practical terms, what did it mean to fight evil in these instances? Can we say that our project of building a just society or our attachment to the ones we love cannot be threatened by death in its various forms? Can we say that we must protect them at the cost of our own life? But if those we love have disappeared, whether victims of hostile forces or of sudden unexpected illness, can we still speak of victory over evil? Would it not be contradictory to proclaim victory for the good? Allende believed she was able to fight the evil that had overtaken her country and her life. But events turned out otherwise. If we look at historic events as well as what happened in her personal life, we would have to say that her hopes were almost completely frustrated. What happened for her was a change in which one evil was replaced by another evil, just as in some situations one good is replaced by another good.

To fight evil one must surely believe that victory is possible. Allende fought with all her strength, imagination, and creativity. In spite of her efforts, the daily wear and tear of life brought a certain acquiescence to the inexorable that forms part of the mystery of human existence. At the end of an event or of a life (and there may be several interpretations of this end), we have to give in to what happened, to this lack of outcome, or rather, to an outcome other than the one for which we had hoped. We give in to what is relative and provisional, to the unforeseeable, or even to what is foreseeable in the evil we have had to accept.

> You have been sleeping for a month now. I don't know how to reach you; I call and call but your name is lost in the nooks and crannies of this hospital. My soul is choked in sand. Sadness is a sterile desert. I don't know how to pray. I cannot string together two thoughts, much less immerse myself in creating a new book. I plunge myself into these pages in an irrational attempt to overcome my terror. I think that perhaps if I give form to this devastation, I shall be able to help you, and myself, and that the meticulous exercise of writing can be

our salvation. Eleven years ago I wrote a letter to my grandfa-
ther to say goodbye to him in death. On this January 8, 1992,
I am writing you, Paula, to bring you back to life.[15]

Here doubt torments Allende. What she writes shows that her
grief is no longer founded in the certitudes of life or the reawaken-
ing of her daughter. Writing becomes a means of salvation: writing
to allay fear, to make sense of what is irrational. Writing to continue to struggle for her daughter's life and for her own life is a
kind of salvation mixed with anguish, suffering, and the fear of
death, a salvation of daily life's tedium in the midst of its sorrows
and pleasures.

There exists within Allende a refusal to despair, or perhaps a
despairing hope that she herself embodies. As she says, at first it is
a desperate hope that makes her write. Then the desperate hope
becomes calmer in the face of stubborn reality. So she continues to
write even when she is now certain that her daughter will not
regain consciousness. She writes for an anonymous audience, or
rather, she writes for herself in search of her own salvation: "I am
no longer writing so when my daughter wakes up she will not feel
so lost, because she is not going to wake up. These are pages Paula
will never read."[16]

Increasingly the author finds she has no answers to her questions. As she looks on her dying daughter, life becomes for her
both miracle and enigma. There are only temporary and incomplete answers. The questions remain always open. Allende writes
of her daughter: "Life is a miracle, and for her it ended abruptly,
without time to say goodbye or settle her accounts, at the moment
of vertiginous, youthful momentum. She was cut off just as she was
beginning to wonder about the meaning of things, and left me the
charge of finding the answer."[17] And finally the expected happens:

Near dawn on Sunday, December 6, after a miraculous night
in which the veils that conceal reality were parted, Paula died.
It was at four in the morning. Her life ended without struggle, anxiety, or pain; in her passing there was only the absolute
peace and love of those of us who were with her. She died in

my arms, surrounded by her family, the thoughts of those absent, and the spirits of her ancestors who had come to her aid.[18]

An assent takes place in Allende's life—not an assent to meaninglessness, but an assent to a meaning other than that which she thought to be the meaning of life and death.[19] The evil of death seems to have transformed her into another person, one who testifies that the human being is this fleeting "mixture" identified by some provisional sense of meaning.

Evil described in a literary or poetic form was also the medium in which Violeta Parra, one of the greatest poets, singers, and folklorists of Chile, sought her salvation. She could not bear prolonging her suffering, and in spite of her art, which gave life to so many people, especially during the military dictatorship, she committed suicide in 1967. The evil she endured was embroiled in the troubled, passionate life of an artist with a political militancy and enormous existential contradictions that she faced during her life. She had a striking intuition about how to struggle against evil—to set traps for it, to fight it by surprising it, to make it afraid.

Here we find a given very dear to popular Latin American culture: one evil must be destroyed by another evil to become a good. One slaps a child who behaves badly to make it a good child. Punishment, in spite of its contradictions, becomes a remedy for restoring good. This is not the law of retaliation (an eye for an eye) but something we encounter in everyday experience.

> If I write this poem
> it is not just to give me pleasure
> but to make evil afraid
> of treason.[20]

In her poetry, so in tune with current language, Parra observes the experience of evil in this world and the ephemeral nature of pleasure. This fragility of pleasure carries a high price—for one minute of pleasure, "a hundred and twenty thousand of pain."

> For the one who leaves this earth,
> death is the end of the world,

with no pain comes
an end to this war.
A dog's life
for one minute of pleasure
and a hundred and twenty thousand of pain.
This is no exaggeration
if the world succeeds in surpassing
the pains of Saint Jobundo.[21]

Parra sees the tragic nature of life, experiences the meaninglessness, the pain, the sadness of existence. Life for a woman sensitive
to the pain of others is a war wherein she must undergo so much
grief for one instant of enjoyment. And for her, no explanation can
convince her and quell her desire to understand why suffering
always overcomes the small moments of happiness.

I do not weep for the pleasure of weeping
But in order to have a little peace.
My tears are like a prayer
that no one wants to hear,
to see and consider
the sad disaster
in all its grandeur,
the lack of virtue,
that is what makes me weep.[22]

For Parra this desire to understand that is never fulfilled is the
source of her suffering, an evil. What she yearns to understand
goes beyond the domestic world, the realm of women. She travels,
works, sings, operates in a public world, hoping to find what she
seeks. Never succeeding in understanding the meaning of her life,
she gives herself over to death, the ultimate boundary of her longing. Is this experience of nonmeaning and despair specific to
women? Surely not. But the way of expressing the pain of living is
different for a woman than for a man.

Eager to take part in the liberation movement of her country,
Parra joined a leftist party. By obeying the rules of the party, paradoxically she experienced the struggle for freedom under a struc-

ture alien to her own freedom—she had to give up her self, her love, to obey the party. This sacrifice is seen as heroic for a man, but not for Parra or other women. After the prison of domesticity, a political party of the left should have laid open a path to freedom, a path for women to enter into the public world. But for many, as for Parra, it was a new route to submission. Ultimately she acknowledged the powerlessness of one woman facing the power of a party, and since she could not find any satisfactory solution, she left.

Her poetry is one of sadness and the enjoyment of momentary happiness. It sings of the fragility of life and its transitory beauty. It is a song of love, describing its traps as well as its marvels. In the end, Violeta Parra's art still nourishes those who believe in justice, liberty, and the delicate beauty of life.

Women's Lack of Education

Sister Juana Inés de la Cruz is another witness to the evil suffered by women. Her torture was the yearning for education, a benefit forbidden to women of her time and social status. This kind of torture is evidence of the many sites and complexities of evil.

Octavio Paz regards Juana Inés de la Cruz, Mexican writer and religious of the Convent of St. Jerome, as the first feminist of Latin America. Even though she lived in the seventeenth century, the term *feminist* current in our time suits her well. Of course, she did not develop feminist theory as we have today, but her life and certain of her works manifest remarkable insights into the inequality of human relationships and the suffering resulting from it. In some ways her life, more than her writing, condemns the oppression of institutions that keep women in a position of inferiority, all in God's name.

So many battles have been waged to enter the realm of knowledge, that eminently male domain reserved for those who by birth have become entitled to access. Great psychological trauma has been inflicted, leading even to a disavowal of one's femininity, in order to enter the enchanted world of male wisdom or simply the field of learning. In New Spain (Mexico) in the seventeenth century, male knowledge, that unique locus of wisdom, was the privilege of an elite convinced of its own superiority, consisting largely of churchmen. De la Cruz had to endure seeing her books burned after so much work—her longing for study reduced to ashes. In the end sickness and death became the lot of this extraordinary woman, who dared to seek knowledge and made every effort to acquire it. This search became her field of battle for equality and justice, where she found creativity and happiness too, but this battlefield was also her death site. An illegitimate child with no social position and many prejudicial labels, she succeeded even at the price of her premature death in entering the world of letters, the path leading to the altar of knowledge she so craved.

To know, study, and ponder certain essential questions like God, human nature, salvation, life and death—these were allotted only to men. Knowledge, science, and politics were male affairs. In a patriarchal society the social division of work and human business is fixed within well-determined limits. We must not go beyond what has been established by God from the beginning of time. In New Spain during de la Cruz's lifetime, women lived without the benefits of education, and if they wanted to acquire them, there was a high price to pay. Only a small minority even tried. New Spain had a large indigenous population. Women directly descended from the Spanish and half-caste women maintained the same model of division in social roles. They regarded domestic duties as their destiny in life, even in convents, where they were not under the thumb of a husband or father. Although they had a certain autonomy relative to their family, women religious manifested submission not only to the male hierarchy but also to the womanly tasks of colonial society. Thus convents replicated the mores of the colonial culture even though, on the inside, the duties, style of life, and domestic responsibilities were different.

Because of this situation and because of her own personal desires, de la Cruz had to become a man symbolically in order to taste the fruit of the tree of knowledge. She had to learn to speak the language of men, to seduce them by her intelligence rather than her beauty or her goodness, just to get the merest public recognition. She became a religious through a desire for knowledge, which attracted her from an early age. The convent was a place where she would be able to try to live her life as an intellectual. It was a way to enter the place of divine knowledge by a feasible and publicly honored path. As she herself says with complete honesty, "I became a religious for this reason even though I knew that this state of life bore with it many things repugnant to my nature, like religious exercises and the company of the community."[23]

De la Cruz was well aware that the world of relationships between men and women was full of ambiguity and that women were always considered more accountable for sins for which they bore only a partial responsibility. A stanza of one of her poems, often quoted by Latin American feminists, is a good expression of this point:

> Ignorant men who accuse
> women idly,
> you don't see that you are the very cause
> of what you accuse them of.[24]

She seems to see clearly the inequality in men's judgments as well as the internal contradiction in their logic. Although she does not often develop that theme in her writings, one finds it in poems and letters defending herself.

De la Cruz did not give up education at the end of her life voluntarily; it was a humiliation imposed by the ecclesiastical authorities responsible for the Inquisition in New Spain. They represented the power of that world of learning to which she aspired, a world that welcomed her as a servant but rejected her as an intellectual, as a being capable of thinking. Likewise, the superiors of the Convent of St. Jerome, who had interiorized the way men think about women and were living out their own internal petty jealousies, became accomplices in the accusation to which she fell victim.

De la Cruz perceived the evil of not being able to pursue her ideal. While she herself did not write about this suffering, commentators wrote on her behalf.[25] She did arrive at her dream of education, and she struggled her whole life to achieve it with the help of the viceroys of Spain, her protectors. But at the very height of her career, she was done in, crushed by the possessors of the good she sought. The men who held power over sacred knowledge did not acknowledge her wisdom and were unable to bear her intrusion into their domain: she threatened them the way Prometheus threatened the gods. They stopped her in the name of God and virtue. In their view, they stopped the aberration of her soul, too preoccupied with knowledge; they checked her wish to transgress the laws of female nature so as to enter the male universe.[26] With no access to her longed-for objective, she accepted the only possible solution: obedience, silence, giving in to death. De la Cruz lived another two years after she was silenced, caring for her Sisters who fell victim to the plague, cleaning the convent, performing household chores considered more suitable for a feminine nature. Drained by suffering and sickness, acknowledging herself to be the "vilest of all," she handed over her body and her dreams to the great Mystery who fashioned her.[27]

What key of interpretation can help us understand this evil suffered by de la Cruz? Will the feminist or hermeneutical concept of gender allow us to comprehend the complexity of this life? I think no key can unlock the richness of her life or of its symbolic force. Even with certain precise historical data, we are dealing with mere attempts at interpretation. No interpretation fully exhausts lived experience. We know that it is always possible to add another and to have some new insight into life.

Scholars studying the work of Juana Inés de la Cruz use various lenses to understand her thought.[28] One approach focuses on her use of ancient Egyptian, Greek, and Roman myths, which is similar to that of other authors of her time. Octavio Paz uses myths as well as psychoanalytic works to help us appreciate the riches and limits of her character. I will use some of this interpretation but only to try to show that it embraces a social organization that is hierarchical and basically male in nature. This means that the concept of gender transcends the interpretation of myth and psychoanalysis, demonstrating the partial nature of interpretations. We cannot escape the inherent limits on interpretation, but we can recognize them in order to accept the richness and the contradictions of these several interpretations.

According to Octavio Paz's hypothesis, de la Cruz, an illegitimate child, had conflicting feelings about her father. The absentee father becomes a subject of idealization and nostalgia, hero or monster. He produced in her a feeling different from the one described in psychoanalytic literature. According to Paz's hypothesis,

> the daughter kills her father and not her mother, and this indicates an inversion of sex and values. A double transgression: to kill the image of one's father and to take on, not the image of the mother, but the masculine image. This masculinization is in turn denied in a second movement of psychic life: Juana Inés converts the phantom of her father into the specter of her husband and she is transformed into a widow. In this way she is identified with her mother—really the widow, although not legally, of Asbaje—and the "masculinization" is changed into "feminization": Juana Inés substitutes herself for her mother.[29]

Further, Octavio Paz believes that one of the archetypes of Juana was Isis, the Egyptian goddess, who appears in her plays and poetry and who is "not only the universal mother of seeds, plants, and animals but the inventor of writing, the mistress of signs."[30]

From Paz's theory we can conclude that what happened to Juana Inés is directly tied to the character of the structure in which she was voluntarily and involuntarily both accomplice and victim. To attempt to understand her through psychoanalysis, inverted in her case, or through a kind of reviving of mythic personages is a valuable approach but limited to a single perspective. In explaining her "misbehavior," perhaps we ought to speak of her longing for freedom instead of her disobedience. Juana Inés violates the rules governing the social division of work and the agreements of her era. She shows thereby the arbitrariness of a system that excludes and punishes in the name of a natural law established by God. In my view, her search for freedom is the aspect to stress, not just the psychological reversals of her personality. To stress inversions could lead us to see de la Cruz through criteria for normality established by the male-dominated field of science and by a culture that gives primacy to men. Instead we ought to underline her desire for freedom, which is translated into a desire for knowledge and a desire to see that knowledge recognized. These two desires seem to be the guiding forces of her story.

De la Cruz does not explicitly develop the theme of liberty in her poems or theatrical works, but it is present like a musical note sounded throughout her writings. Disobedience, the expression of a possible freedom, allowed her to become an artist and poet and was the means of salvation she employed.

Women's Lack of Worth

Not being valued is another cause of evil for women. We are not speaking here about their worth in relation to men but as women in themselves. Some women have value only as objects—objects of enjoyment or of revenge, objects of pleasure or of hate. Women-objects have difficulty in regarding themselves as autonomous, as *subjects* who can guide their destiny even while taking note of what is not under their control. Age is of little account in becoming an object. In some situations, especially under bad economic conditions, females begin to be treated as objects at an early age. Sexual tourism and traffic in young girls for houses of prostitution are examples. Girls are not worth anything in themselves, only as merchandise for men.

The journalist Gilberto Dimenstein, who has reported on the traffic of young girls sold into prostitution in Brazil, writes of this deplorable scene with all its ambiguities and contradictions. The majority of these young women, who are between the ages of twelve and eighteen, are caught in the trap of work. They are promised honest work to help them get out of poverty. They do indeed get work but of such a sort that it would be very difficult to leave without outside help. Their employment leaves its pitiful

mark on their whole life. A man speaking to other men, Dimenstein describes the sentiments men have and shares the expressions
used when it is announced that new girls are coming to a town or
city.

> When a "sealed" girl—the expression used for a virgin—
> arrives, the town gets advance word. Who will give the best
> price for the right of being first? Men get together in the
> room. Dalva, the madam, brings the girl in, looking good,
> made up, wearing a new dress, making overtures. Bids begin
> to pour in up to the highest rate, generally offered by the sons
> of wealthy landowners. The next day this is the topic of con-
> versation among rich young men. Deflowering a girl is a sign
> of social status.[31]

A little further in the same book the writer goes on to show how
the arrival of new girls provides a motif for a village celebration.
"When new girls arrive in port, there is a celebration, and that
evening men vie for the privilege of being the first to taste 'fresh
meat.'"[32] We may ask, Would this be a celebration for everyone?

There is a turnover in this kind of market. In prostitution girls
are soon worn out by overwork, deprivation, and all kinds of dis-
eases. Their bodies are worth only as much as clients value this
merchandise. When the product is no longer pleasing, they are
sent to a poorer region to go on with their work. This is the mer-
ciless law of the market. Bodies of young women become game-
boards, things to enjoy and argue over. And all this is considered
normal, natural, part of the culture, and ultimately necessary for
men's health. Feast, festival, competition, exchange of money—
all take place over the bodies of young women. They offer their
bodies to follow the course of a celebration, to be used and then
discarded.

To grow in social status is considered a benefit for many men,
and ownership over women's bodies is a sign of social privilege.
How can a benefit for some people be considered an evil for others? How can the same actions have such different meanings, to
say nothing of contradictions, according to whose body it is and

whose understanding? Why does this disparity of good and evil happen? Why this incongruity in existence itself? We could answer that many people affirm certain behavior as ethical for themselves or those they love but not necessarily for others. In the case we are considering, the ethics of a certain social class befits its own direct interests. It allows the exploitation of the bodies of the poor and demands respect for the bodies of the rich. It respects white bodies more and black bodies less. It uses different weights and measures according to who is playing the game.

Value, meaning here the value of one's entire self, opens a new window for hearing and considering the evil endured by women. Women who by their economic condition are not worth very much interiorize the worthlessness society bestows on them as their heritage and do so early in their childhood. It is difficult to get out of this mind set unless some "savior" comes to their aid. Thus young girls, slaves to an unjust social structure characterized by devaluing one sex over the other, dream of a prince, a hero who will save them. In their longing and imagination they are the actresses in the television soap operas and radio dramas in which a happy ending always comes to those who follow the rules. This happy ending is their whole horizon of hope, especially for those just starting out in the trade. This is how one young woman puts it: "I am looking for a husband. Some girls and women have become high society when they got to know their husband in the place of prostitution. I have great hopes."[33]

While girls are in prostitution, they hope to escape. But for some their aspiration is to get in, to be accepted as a prostitute, especially when they are over twenty-five. After twenty-five, women are already shopworn, too old to please clients. The female body is merchandise with a short shelf life, refurbished when the stock runs out. It obeys the laws of the market with its own logic, a logic of consumerism and of excluding and oppressing some to the benefit of others.

Maids who work in family homes experience the same devaluing of their persons. Their bodies are also mere objects and have no value except to serve others. The words of Lenira, a maid living for a long time in Recife, are clear and touching: "No one wants to be a maid today, no one considers it, no one values it—not society, no individual, not even those of us who are maids."[34] Domestics themselves accept household work as a last resort in order to survive. When there is a way to get out of it, even for a lower salary, they do. Being a maid means a kind of personal recognition of the inability of a woman to do anything else with her life.

Lenira gives us a glimpse of her life when she says to a journalist: "The dogs in the house are worth more than we are. The lady of the house respects her dog. We're not worth respecting; we are good only to work. I didn't want to work in a house and consider myself lower than a dog. I wanted to be considered a professional, a person who rendered service, who was competent."[35] Everyone seeks to be esteemed, and when one is not, life is worth nothing. This is an aspect of existence common to many women who are always trying to survive in a society so elitist that it refuses to recognize them as professional, worthy, and competent.

"I Am Black, but I Am Beautiful," or the Evil Attributed to Skin Color

In the Americas, one source of trouble for women of African descent is their skin color. The dominant culture establishes a hierarchy based on skin color. To be a woman is already a problem, but to be female and black is to suffer double jeopardy, just as to be female and black and poor is to have triple jeopardy. What madness affects this issue of color? Why are some colors associated with evil and unhappiness and others with good and satisfaction? How did the symbolism of evil come to be tied to colors? Why have our differences become a source of inferiority, prejudice, and exclusion?

These questions have no answers, but we must raise them nonetheless in order to revise our judgment about the presence of certain evils we have come to accept as natural. In solidarity with my African sisters, far and near, I want to echo their cry. I have some inkling of their sorrow. I recognize their suffering even though I do not experience their distress and marginalization.

Theology has never considered discrimination because of skin color to be suffering. European theologians have never undergone this suffering as their own or as a part of Christian ethics or as a fundamental element in the quest for justice. The existence of dark-skinned slaves, men and women alike, was historically of no great concern to Christian ethics. Only in the twentieth century did we begin to listen to the voices of African theologies and African American communities in their thirst for freedom, respect, and recognition. As the African American theologian Delores Williams says:

> Africa, a source of black American heritage, has been and often still is depicted in many American sources as a wilderness continent inhabited by "subhuman savages," not civilized according to European (white) standards. Blackness is looked upon with disdain. In North America popular culture, religion, science and politics have worked together to assign permanent negative value to the color black. This has led to the formation of an American national consciousness that considers black frightening, dangerous and/or repulsive—especially when this is the color of human bodies.[36]

This repulsion based on color, often unconsidered, also crosses the culture of Latin America. Generally speaking, what is white is close to good and justice while what is black is close to evil, tragedy, bad situations, the devil. In the northeast of Brazil it is common not to allow black children to dress as angels in religious feasts, especially those of the Virgin. No black child could ever crown the Virgin Mary on the last day of May. Along the same lines we should consider popular sayings about people of African descent and particularly about the sexuality of black women. Such language is present in daily life in Latin American culture. Astonishingly, black women are thought of as being especially close to nature or the wilderness, understood here as some uncivilized place beyond all rationality. Thus in Brazil mulattos are considered the best merchandise to develop sexual tourism.[37]

In her book *The Bluest Eye* Toni Morrison tells the story of a young black child who prays to have blue eyes.[38] She wants to be considered beautiful and to be accepted. When we examine the criteria for beauty established by our Western society, we discover that beauty often becomes a question of power. Beauty is subject to the laws of the market; it is often tied to profit and to ethnic conflicts. We may ask again: Why this negative attitude to the color black, and especially when it concerns skin color? Probably no single answer to this question exists, but what is clear is a hierarchical arrogance deriving particularly from the power of white people compared to that of black people. But what is also striking is the way many black people themselves, both women and men, have interiorized this negative evaluation of their skin, this connection of black with something bad. On the one hand, we note a consent to the injustices produced by the culture, even if, on the other, there are more and more movements of black consciousness springing up everywhere in Latin America.

In the United States, most black people know that they have to "act white" in order to be accepted or valued. In my country I often hear: "He/she is black but he/she has a white soul," and "he/she is black but well educated." Having a white soul is the way to be assimilated as white in our societies. The white model is the only one worthy of being called human, good, and educated. Even at the level of religious expression in everyday life this difference sometimes is forcefully manifested. People will say, for example, that God loves everyone but takes pity on blacks. Why is pity added to love? We know that it has historical roots: it was introduced into our culture from the time of slavery. God permitted the existence of black slaves and took pity on them by inviting them to become Christians. In this sense, we could speak of a theology and ethic for white people and a different one for black people.

In our human relationships a kind of pathology is expressed in an attitude of superiority over those considered inferior. Such behavior is not confined to colonial times but continues as a form of control, of economic and cultural exploitation by one color over another. There is also less acknowledgment of guilt when black populations or their territories are destroyed or when a black person is assassinated. Where black people are concerned, it is as though we are dealing with matters of less importance and value. This is what North American writers call "white racial narcissism."[39] We are proud of being white, of belonging to the civilization that is capable of conquering the world. Others, black men and black women, are people of less worth, and so we feel less guilty when misfortunes happen to them.

Moreover, in the Americas to be a black woman means undergoing not only the evil of hierarchy among races but the hierarchy of sex among black people. It is this aspect of oppression within the African American community that Alice Walker reveals in her remarkable book *The Color Purple.* Written as a journal addressed to God and using the language and grammar of a poor black woman, this book shows us the riches of Celie's life. Celie wants to understand what is happening, so she asks God the cause of her torments. Her questions make us think of the book of Job.

> Dear God,
>
> I am fourteen years old. . . . I have always been a good girl. Maybe you can give a sign letting me know what is happening to me.
>
> Last spring after little Luscious come I heard them fussing. He was pulling on her arm. She say It too soon, Fonso, I ain't well. . . .
>
> He never had a kine word to say to me. Just say You gonna do what your mammy wouldn't.[40]

Here we have the invective of her mother's companion, incapable of accepting her sickness and uneasiness that lead her to refuse sexual relations for the time being. He decides to use the youngster for his manly "needs."

> Dear God,
>
> He beat me today cause he say I winked at a boy in church. I may have got somethin in my eye but I didn't wink. I don't even look at mens. That's the truth.[41]

Some women of African descent suffer devaluation even in their own milieu by reason of being a woman. Women serve men. They are brought up to serve them, and this education is a source of submission and unhappiness. To try to think differently and to change the rules of the dominant male culture is one of the most important challenges to establishing the worth and autonomy of black-skinned women.

Women's "Evils" Seen through the Lens of Justice

Testimony of women like Sister Juana Inés de la Cruz, Isabel Allende, and the other women mentioned above invites us to enlarge our perspective on the problem of evil and to adopt a new interpretive approach. Such an interpretation will become clearer when we apply the concept of gender in the following chapter. Nevertheless, it is important to highlight systematically several aspects of their testimony in order to create a foundation for our interpretation.

Each witness has taught us something about her life. Because aspects of their testimony are echoed in our own experience, we can, using critical distance and certain tools of interpretation, accept their stories as factual retelling of their experience of evil. While attempting to preserve objectivity, we must acknowledge that by speaking of another's experience, we are mingling our own with it. Whatever is said will never be able to contain exactly what has been lived. Nevertheless, even as my own words intervene in these testimonies, I use them to denounce evil as I seek the light of justice and solidarity.

In looking at the story of Ruku in *Nectar in a Sieve,* I note that she never mentions her own feelings of grief as she tells her story. Like the others, she shows us the tragic fabric of a human life, especially the life of a poor woman. She seems to be walking a narrow path with an abyss on either side and with unforeseen misfortunes looming. In her story we recognize the rigidness of a stratified world in which each person's worth is reckoned by possessions and social rank. Here a hierarchy determines that women's rights are not the same as men's in the daily give-and-take of human relations. The experience of Ruku's daughter is another factor in the family's struggle just to stay alive. Facing her brother's death from starvation, she offers herself to "shameless men" for the price of rice. An evil action or a Christlike one? The answer depends on the interpreter. Those sensitive to human distress see this gesture of a young girl as Christlike, salvific, loving. The shame and evil she bears in her body give way to the joy of seeing a faint smile on the lips of her little brother.

Is there any way of better describing the evils present in the lives of these women? In my view, the evils stem from lack of ownership, but that is not the whole story. Poverty triggers the evil of powerlessness and worthlessness. They all come together in the anthropological disaster of being female and further in the mystery of human evil. Not only does self-contempt take over, but so does an utter inability to change a dreadful situation. Thus poverty intersects with other ills and demands a concern for mercy and justice.

What does the experience of powerlessness mean in the lives of the women mentioned here? Living as women do in the slums of Brazil is not at all the same as the experiences described by Isabel Allende or Violeta Parra. Powerlessness takes on different faces in women's lives. It is characterized by a certain resistance to change, an insensitivity toward others' troubles, immobility in one's own suffering, inability to find some alternative. For women in the ghettos it is having to face the deadly daily reality of finding the wherewithal to live. "When there is water, there is no soap. When there is soap, there is no water." This would be a trifling matter to generals or heads of state or even to political analysts who worry about lack of power. "Today I was lucky. There was a lot of trash in the streets." Collecting trash confers the power to eat: who among politicians would set the standard so low? But that is where power is found when survival is at stake.

Evil for Carolina Maria de Jesus means people *not* throwing trash on the street. Evil is *not* having the garbage necessary for her livelihood and that of her children. Paper mixed in with garbage is power for her.

Powerlessness for Isabel Allende is connected more closely to watching her daughter die than to facing the dictatorial regime under which she lived and which lives now in her memory. The dictatorship has fallen, and her daughter is dead. For Allende the evil of powerlessness is evident in the insurmountable limits of existence. And the evil that is present is not moral, an ethical failure, but embodied in the finitude of human existence, the evil everyone experiences at the loss of a loved one. Ultimately we are all caught in this kind of grief; in contrast, in the case of other events, there might be some other possibility to avoid an experience of evil. Violeta Parra's suffering is of the same kind. Human beings endlessly yearn for love and justice, a desire that brings grief. And here too the experience of powerlessness takes on a special shape in women's lives.

Sister Juana Inés de la Cruz presents a woman's experience of being denied access to knowledge, but that experience is intermingled with other factors. Having no access to an education is an evil peculiar to women and to the poor. Even before they acknowledge that they do not know this or that, society has already judged their intelligence. To be female or poor in a patriarchal and hierarchical society is almost synonymous with ignorance. De la Cruz always dreamed of education, the power of knowledge, the value it would confer on her. Her life became the battlefield for knowledge. How could this passion for education become an evil? Or how could it bring disaster upon her?

Human wisdom enters into a power struggle between the sexes. An analysis of gender reveals that control over knowledge and the accepted wisdom is truly men's power and privilege. Women are intruders, usurpers of something not belonging to them. They do wrong when they desire to know, and as an answer to this wrong, society must restore harmony by chastisement, silence, torture, or death. In this way the hierarchy of the world and of humanity is maintained.

The human person builds his or her own humanity through recognition of his or her self-worth, personality, and uniqueness. When their worth is unacknowledged, people experience evil. This melancholy experience of being the least regarded occurs particularly in places of prostitution, where young girls full of dreams of happiness are assailed by the harshness of life and by their bodies being reduced to merchandise. Contrary to popular belief, young girls often dream of the evil of selling their bodies as a path to their good. Good and evil are mixed up and feed off one another. In the daily routine, evil seems to be the absence of life's possibilities, the violence with which they are treated, the insecurity they feel, the lack of warmth and affection that characterizes their existence.

What more is there to say of this evil? How do we classify it, pardon it, exterminate it? Of all created beings, humans are the only ones capable of committing the most subtle evils and, even more astonishing, of claiming that they are good. Humans fight and kill each other because of skin color. The irrational human evils include racism, ethnic violence, and all kinds of prejudices. People of African descent are invited to deny their color and their values to become white in order to be accepted in a world that marginalizes them. Just as there is one sex that is normative, so in the West there is one skin color that is normative. And this white norm becomes an evil if one is born black or brown. From this norm arise impossible desires—the wish for the blue eyes of the white doll. From this norm springs the contempt for difference and the poverty that is tied to skin color. A feminist phenomenology of evil acknowledges the complexity and intersection of various evils, those always before us, in us, around us. The evidence invites us to theologize about them and to discover the complicity of our theologies in maintaining injustice.

My Own Story

In general, when theology or philosophy speaks of evil, it offers a discourse on evil, that is, a reflection on evil observed or experienced or witnessed in society. It deals with some concrete observable phenomenon. The evil is something recognized as immoral, disgusting, pernicious, destructive. The evil thus exposed becomes an object of denunciation and reproach. Even so, the description of this evil does not necessarily manifest the personal experience of the one who has undergone it.

In the beginning of this chapter I used the phenomenological method to try to allow women's experience of evil to speak for itself. That experience was, in a sense, laid out before me. I had selected instances. If I showed anything of my own preferences or commitment, my own experience of evil did not appear. I have recounted the testimony of other women; I have relayed their sorrow and heard their avowal indirectly. Now I want to focus on another form of the expression of evil, still following the path laid open by phenomenology, by telling a personal story. The feminist movement, particularly in Latin America, has used this tactic to help women express in their own words what has happened to them and to realize the value of their own experience.

As a way of recounting, beginning with oneself and one's burden, suffering, difficulty, hope, and joy—that is, personal storytelling— help us discover the complexity of influential psychological, social, economic, cultural, and religious factors. Starting with one's own story, one comes to see a broader picture, placing oneself in a particular time and culture. This is not a matter of absolutizing individual experience but of showing how each person exists in relation with others, with the larger world, with the earth, and with the whole ecosystem. Because of this living relation, we continue to create what we call good and what we call evil.

This kind of reflection is not an abstract act: it takes one's own experience as matter for thought, as a book to be studied, as a school in which one can develop personhood by using certain tools. This method receives little appreciation from those who advocate the scientific method, in which the subject must be set apart and emotion plays no part in what is called objective knowledge. But for some feminist groups subjectivity, emotion, sensitivity, and interconnection among different levels of existence are fundamental to knowledge. I share this perspective. For the rest of this chapter I will proceed subjectively, considering certain aspects of evil in my own experience. I am doing this despite the uneasiness and reluctance I feel. In a methodological exercise designed to test the efficacy of a feminist phenomenology, I am using myself as an object of reflection in solidarity with other marginalized women who use this method.

Enormous difficulties come with using a text about oneself. One has to reveal oneself to an unknown audience. This is my case. It arouses a double malaise in me: first, because of the very nature of revealing oneself in writing, a revelation without a reciprocal disclosure; also because of the knowledge that the wounds inflicted on my life are minimal compared to what other women have suffered. Mine pale in significance before what so many women have shared about their daily heartaches. My suffering, even if it causes me pain, cannot be measured against the burden my sisters have to carry in different parts of the country and the world. While there is no comparison, it is true that, since I live by choice in a poor neighborhood, I cannot help feeling the burden of my own privileges.

Speaking of the evil in one's own life is like St. Augustine's personal confession in which he takes himself as an object of reflection and asks himself the same questions posed to others. The context and the purpose are different, but the confession, or simply personal sharing, offers rich elements for consideration. We know that each personal experience of evil, involving different elements, makes it more difficult to understand evil's complex character. It is like a labyrinth with no exit. One is slave and free at the same time, living life's paradox without satisfactory answers, declaring that this is good today, that that may be bad tomorrow. One event is not experienced in the same way by different people even if they live in the same conditions. This makes speaking about evil in general and my own personal experience more difficult.

My comments on my own experience, therefore, derive from memory and interpretation. By telling my story I simultaneously reveal and conceal myself. I tell one thing, and I hide so many others! I do not have a total grasp of the events I describe or of my own analysis. My telling is incomplete and full of ambiguity, an interpretation of the facts of my life or a reading of the past that can be unjust toward others who were with me. This is the delicate condition of all human speech that we must accept in its richness and complexity. This is the result of fully accepting the good and the evil life offers us. The threads of life form a fabric according to each one's personality, and they produce different results.

How to begin? Which events? What choice? I will begin not with a chronological review of my whole life but with key moments that will point out the uniqueness of my experience and perhaps allow others to recognize similarities to their own lives. Thus I need to share events meaningful to me. I will select certain ones, knowing that they are distant from the telling and that all events are woven into the fabric of my present life, causing me to be who I am. Conscious of these limitations, I hand over my experiences to the reader.

Born Female

To have been born a girl was hard: my family, who immigrated to Brazil from the Near East, was expecting a boy. My parents' disappointment has always been with me like a wound. I am not, because of my sex, what they wanted me to be. I could never realize their hopes, their dreams, their pride. I am only a woman; in their culture, that means dependent, submissive, lacking the possibility of continuing the family name. My father could never hope to have a son since he was already old when I was born. "A girl, only a girl—through what mysterious plans of God do we have a girl, we who so wanted a boy? There is nothing to do but to accept this fate we cannot change." These are the words I often heard, although spoken lightly or in jest by my parents and relatives.

As I grew up marked by this fate, this family frustration always meant for me a struggle to prove my value since I was "only" a girl. In some way I had to overcome what they considered the worthlessness in me. But it was not evident that a girl could have any value in herself. On the contrary, in the culture in which I was raised a girl gains value when she is obedient to her father and mother, to her husband, or simply to her family. She takes on value by her beauty, the domestic services she performs, her ability to be an excellent mother and manager of the household. Men have value in themselves, in their autonomy, in their efforts to make something of themselves and to be socially recognized. But as for me, since I was not male, I looked for some worth in myself. Thus I was often accused of being insubordinate, of wasting my time with books and lectures, things absolutely useless for women. To be myself and to have some value in myself became for me a sort of pleasure and pride, a challenge and adventure, but at the same time a cross difficult to bear because it always ran against the grain. I had to bear complaints at home as I sought some kind of status in the world of academics, in a world different from my family. This world presented itself as the place where I could finally find my own worth.

The choice to enter a religious order was a logical result of finding value in myself. At first glance, that view may seem a contradiction, especially today when women's religious institutions are criticized for being patriarchal. But for me it was a path to justice and freedom, a place where I could live gospel values without the constraints of my native culture. This choice led me to leave home and, as a result, to grieve for years over my parents' lack of understanding. My desire for freedom has produced guilt that has left its own deep traces in me. Why all this suffering? I ask myself every day. Why should my happiness have to come at the cost of the unhappiness of my parents? Why should my dreams of liberty and self-worth have to mean the death of their own dreams? Reflection on these contradictions in life is part of my daily bread, even after years of happy perseverance in this path.

The Influence of Matriarchs

It is clear to me, feminist that I have become, that the strength of the matriarchs in my family proves the worth of women.[42] While these women—my maternal grandmother, my mother, and my aunts—had a great deal of courage in dealing with their lives and the lives of their children, however, their courage was still prisoner to a cultural system that clearly delineated their role as women. I also lived a contradiction: I loved them dearly, and at the same time I did not want to imitate them. Their courage always impressed me, as did their fidelity to duty and their remarkable capacity for self-renunciation. But it aroused in me both admiration and silent criticism, an uneasiness in the face of such examples.

They were brave in their submission to a system of cultural values in which women, even very capable ones who took good care of their households and their children, always had to make a public show of their dependence on their husbands or their sons. Sometimes their courage made me feel bad, provoked pity, or aroused rebellion in me and a desire for some nameless freedom. I suspected that something was stifling their development. I did not know how to address it even though I always suspected their unhappiness. I suffered with them, and I suffered from the fear of reproducing in my own life the misery I saw in theirs. I suffered in silence, afraid to reveal my feelings, which were so different from the tradition in which I was brought up.

I thought I was the only one who felt this way and did not share my thoughts even with my sisters, who seemed more or less content to follow this model. I lived the evil of wishing for a different world—I dreamed of my freedom; I yearned to struggle against social injustice; in short, I wanted what seemed forbidden to a daughter of immigrants. This struggle permeated my adolescence and youth, making me dream of another music, another dance in which dancers could follow the music of their own bodies, their own hearts, their own dreams. And this evil, the origin of my dreams, is still present in the various ways in which I do my daily tasks. My evil mixes in with my good and causes me grief.

Living as a Foreigner in My Own Country

Thousands of men and women today, for different reasons, have to look for some place to live outside their native lands. At first glance, there is nothing extraordinary in this experience. It is not directly mine, but I have suffered its consequences because of my parents' situation. In this ordinary experience, common to so many, I see the singularity of my life and also find evil.

In this reflection I discuss women's experience, starting from my own as a daughter of immigrants in a country seemingly democratic, where it would appear all people have a chance to make their own destiny. Where lies the evil in this situation more and more common in our society? What is this evil I am mentioning? What has been my own experience of it? Why has it been an evil for me when it has been a good for so many others? We experience some things as evil without being certain that they are bad. Evil is a connection experienced in different ways and difficult to understand. Subjectivity plays an important role since in some ways it determines the intensity of the evil and its characterization as evil.

I have always felt I belonged to my country, while still feeling like a foreigner. Since my infancy I have not known any other country as my native land, even though my parents shared their memories and their homesickness. Often I heard people say that we were strangers, as if to emphasize our opposition to Brazilian manners and culture. But Brazil is my country. As the daughter of foreigners, I have developed the fear of not being accepted—a fear often present in my life. I was afraid that children or teenagers would make fun of me because of my parents' accent. I always wanted to protect myself, to protect my parents, to hide them, not to speak about their country, their social situation, their culture, their language, their accent. I had to hide the Near East in me and to present an acceptable appearance, to be like everybody else. I had to be Eastern Latin American without knowing how. What particular event sparked in me this fear? In all honesty, I cannot say; I do not know, I do not remember, and I search in vain. But the fear does exist under my skin, in my body, in my thought.

What an evil, what malaise, what a curse to carry within me the division of two cultural worlds, two languages, to love both and not want to be repudiated by either! What wealth I would say today—but what a trial I lived through yesterday. What grief, tears, and wounds any time I felt the least scoffing at my dual cultural background. What pain at every childish mocking of foreigners' accents, of Arabs, so much so that it seems that every foreigner belongs to my family. I have lived through the evil of difference, knowing all the while how important and necessary difference is. I lived this evil even in my religious devotions. I had trouble accepting as valid the Eastern liturgies in which my parents participated. I considered them sinful, gravely offensive to God. And this opinion was reinforced at school in religion classes. I lived contradictions and sufferings with no solution. Basically I believed that the West was always right, that the religious at my school were more intelligent than my parents, that the priests who preached at retreats were the wisest in the world, and that the simplest thing would be for me to be totally in tune with their music. I had to prefer it to what I heard at home.

Life has shown me other positions and has led me to grow up from my youthful judgments. But there are always old traces that remain, memories that come back to me and bring me once again the bitter taste of this past that lives in me.

Being a Woman Theologian of Liberation

What a contradictory evil! How to bear being a woman theologian and, still more, a theologian of liberation? What a bizarre suffering! My trouble as a theologian began with a certain independence of thought. Independent research, looked upon as a good, has brought evil to me. As long as I echoed the ideas of others, there was no conflict. I could serve as a professor of theology and philosophy; that is, I could prepare my courses, using books of theology and philosophy written by men, and I never had a problem. I was highly appreciated and considered a competent professor.

But the season for ripe fruit came, and with it the wish and the desire to say my own word. Independence led me to live a considerable distance from my colleagues, mostly men. One reason for maintaining this distance was my attachment to a feminist perspective. Such a perspective was often considered a problem of the first world trying to influence and coopt us. But my experience working with different groups of women, especially women from the grassroots, showed me that they had something special to consider, a specific oppression experienced by women.

In my view, the oppression of women was not some addendum or just one more theme for theology. It was at the heart of the unjust organization of our societies, an expression of our human sin touching every aspect of existence. What I was saying was in some way the same as what the Latin American male theologians were saying when they spoke of liberation. According to them, liberation was not a Latin American theme tacked on to classic theology. Liberation was the very substance of all theology: in short, liberation and theology should be correlative terms. In order to make my own thought clearer, I would look to Gustavo Gutiérrez's book that serves as the basis for all Latin American liberation theology. Even now his work comes to mind in the midst of these memories and reflections: "The theology of liberation offers us not so much a new theme for reflection as a *new way* to do theology. Theology as critical reflection on historical praxis is a liberating theology, a theology of the liberating transformation of the history of mankind and also therefore that part of mankind—gathered into *ecclesia*—which openly confesses Christ."[43]

Similarly, I would say that feminism, or the marginalization of women, is not just one more theme but that the appearance of women on the public stage of history had to change the very structure of the theological enterprise, taking this new problematic into account. Given the "explosion of women in the midst of the explosion of the poor," as feminists of the third world were saying, it is no longer possible to maintain the same trends of thought or to repeat the same theological formulas. Something very deep within the human person was beginning to awaken. And that necessitated a more inclusive theology, one that took account of different experiences of and approaches to the mystery of God, a theology that elaborated Christology in broader and less sexist categories than had existed up till now.

Feminism, or more specifically, the emergence of women as a new historical subject on the national and international stage, demanded a new theological coherence as well as a new biblical hermeneutic. The concept of gender (discussed in further detail in chapter 2) helped me understand how deeply a hierarchical, dualistic structure was embedded in our theology, so integrally as to become almost its essence, its specificity. Moreover, I noticed how slow theology was to change inasmuch as it upholds the hierarchical structure directly or indirectly and excludes even groups that are Christian.

I often heard that I was not really a theologian but a philosopher, because I held the title of doctor of philosophy and not doctor of theology. For some people this distinction explained the waywardness of my thought. It would seem that the academic title decides whether discoveries of thought are or are not legitimate. This is true also for men, I know, but for women the judgment is harsher and more cutting. I have often heard it said that women are only one subject among others in theology, and that today it is a fashionable subject. Often too I have heard that the theological claims of women have no basis in tradition. But what tradition is that? Must we, while keeping intact the good things of our patriarchal tradition, cling to its harmful aspects and forget the primacy of justice and love? Must we lack respect for the present in the name of the tradition of the past? Must we always glorify the past, the traditions of the fathers, as if their thought were to be useful for every situation and for all cultures?

I have always wanted to respect the tradition of the fathers, but not to absolutize it or to consider it as the sole path to truth or as the parameter for all Christian experience. Feminism has made me see the gaps in the tradition and has reminded me that what passed as a common tradition for all Christianity is, in fact, part of a larger and more complex tradition.

My past struggles still form part of my present reality. Undoubtedly feminist theology has succeeded in opening certain cracks in the male dogmatic structure. Concretely, when we speak of that structure we mean that both church dogma and current theology not only concentrate on male figures but also derive their formulations based on men's experience. We need only recall, for example, that Christian thought has always affirmed in theory that men and women are equally made in the image of God, but in practice women cannot represent God. Men do. For St. Augustine, for example, man is the image of God normatively, but woman is only secondarily.[44] It is striking how many official texts of the Catholic church insist on the maternal role of women and the governing power of men, conferred on them by Christ. This dogmatic theology, quite apart from even traditional dogma, leaves no room for women to be worthwhile in and of themselves or to speak aloud their experience and their observations.[45] Nevertheless, advances are being made, even though we are far from a due respect for women and for all the other beings of the earth.

The Transcendence and Immanence of Evil

I have no desire to analyze or reinterpret the words *transcendence* and *immanence,* but they remind me of something beyond my understanding and my action, something always present despite my desire and effort to oppose it. It seems the reality of being human cannot be called human without this transcendence and immanence of evil. They are constitutive of the human being just as are goodness and the quest for justice. On this subject, my experience helps my thinking in a feverish effort to understand what I have trouble understanding. I am overcome by the feeling of being plunged into an adventure full of uncertainty and of living in a time of evil. What a contradictory statement for one who hopes to live out her days in justice and solidarity! This feeling is not all-consuming, leaving me unaware of the beauty of life and the countless acts of charity and solidarity I witness. It does not drive me to a hopeless pessimism, but it does fill me with a perplexity about life and its lovely fragility.

I have always heard and read and listened to discussions of the transcendence and immanence of good as if there were some good reality, at best an Other who contained all goodness within. The transcendence and immanence of good have always been presented as an assurance that good and justice will one day prevail. What does not yet exist has the possibility of becoming. Goodness, justice, and even happiness exist in some beyond that is difficult to grasp. Every day someone claims justice for tomorrow, the fullness of love for some later date, happiness for all eternity.

In the 1970s, the golden age of liberation theology, the victory of the good, God's victory, or the coming of the kingdom meant the arrival of a just society (socialism), where each person would be respected for his or her own dignity. Gustavo Gutiérrez comes to mind because of the witness of his life and his influence: "From the viewpoint of faith, the motive which in the last instance moves Christians to participate in the liberation of oppressed peoples and exploited social classes is the conviction of the radical incompatibility of evangelical demands with an unjust and alienating society. They feel keenly that they cannot claim to be Christians without a commitment to liberation."[46] At that time the struggle was clearly defined; the social evil was identified. We knew what it meant to be Christians in the world. We knew how to bring about justice and good for everyone. This clarity about the combat burned within me.

But today everything has changed profoundly. These are quite other times. For instance, in the book mentioned above, Gustavo Gutiérrez mentions several times in a positive way the work of Fernando Henrique Cardoso, the president of the Republic of Brazil. Today we live in a situation beyond our former hopes and dreams. This same president has adopted a neoliberal economy and has abandoned his earlier socialist dreams. Life these last years in Brazil and elsewhere in Latin America has made me experience what I dare to call "the transcendence and immanence of evil." It is not that there exists some evil being, as might be described in dualistic God-talk. Nor is it a new Manichaeism. But it is as if some ingredient has infiltrated everywhere and can be called "evil." It has the potential to destroy human relationships, our affinity with the earth, life in all its forms. This is not only a comment on human weakness but an observation of a kind of net that surrounds us in the very air we breathe, of a "sea" in which we move. This experience of realizing that almost all our solutions are, in fact, the result of a lesser evil or of some other type of evil frightens me. Sometimes I think of evil as though it were leaven in dough, hence the difficulty of separating it from the whole. Some Gospel passages suggest to me the presence of evil as keenly as they suggest the presence of good, and this urges me to new paths of reflection and action.

I am well aware of the limits of the human condition, so admirably analyzed by Paul Ricoeur in his *Philosophy of the Will*,[47] but this is something different rearing up and grabbing hold of the human person and the ecosystem. And it is appearing not like some theory of evil or the analysis of a particular situation but like some ingredient ever-present in our daily routine. Sometimes I have the impression that justice consists of isolated acts that contain the least evil. When it comes to relations between men and women, the concept of gender can help our understanding, but it too seems caught in the same net, in the same atmosphere of instability. It has been taken over by exclusionary powers and by our personal sense of revenge.

From my experience of dwelling in a poor section of Camarigibe in Brazil, where I am only one citizen trying to live with a sense of justice and respect toward my neighbors and my environment, the transcendence and immanence of evil strike me every day. *Transcendence* means that evil overtakes us more completely than good, or evil is always present in daily routine. When I see a young mother with four children, abandoned by her husband and having to leave her youngsters in a tiny room facing the street, with bars almost like a prison, so she can go to work; when I see that there are no schools for children; when I see children brawling in the streets, committing little thefts and sometimes crimes, easy prey for drug traffickers; when I surprise myself by being afraid of children, of their violence; when I see a neighbor set fire to another neighbor's stall out of jealousy and competition over trade; when I see my neighbor, who beats his wife and abuses her in public; when I see the carelessness of my neighbors, ignoring the common good, throwing garbage in the street; when I see dirty water coming out of our faucets; when I feel powerless and ignorant as to how to use my own abilities in my neighborhood, suffering becomes my daily bread, and I feel in my own skin the transcendence and immanence of evil.

More than an intellectual treatise, this is an experience, a gut feeling that invades my entire being. In my body, my thought, and my prayer I live in this reality I call "the transcendence and immanence of evil." This thing that destroys is there, omnipresent, taking different concrete form in the most varied situations. I live in my own skin the contradiction of the good news of Jesus, which has no suitable ground for being sown, no possibility of being effectively lived out.

The good we do is often motivated by the affliction and destruction around us. Good is the name for that fragile reality that produces a certain sense of well-being, a certain situation that we call justice, a certain temporary happiness. It is like a delicate flower always in danger of dying. In the popular culture of northeastern Brazilians, who are deeply influenced by African religions, there is agreement that one must pay attention to the gods in charge of evil. Even though they are not stronger in the hierarchy than those who take care of good, they still have a great deal of power. They are present in daily life just as are those who represent good. That is why they must be honored so that they will not produce evil. These beliefs are beginning to have more and more credence among grassroots communities because, among other reasons, people need answers that Roman Catholicism can no longer provide.

All this evidence gives me food for thought on the question of evil. Within this present work I do not think it possible to develop a theological theory about these divinities and powers. I think that we must simply develop an inclusive anthropological phenomenology, that is, one that includes the environment, as well as our bodies, as a place affected by good and evil. I am thinking of a different "geography" and a different "history" of good and evil. In this sense, I am envisioning a blend in which it is impossible to separate clearly the various ingredients. I am thinking of a different religious education, which would set in relief the ambiguous and inclusive character of life itself.

When I speak of the transcendence and immanence of evil, I am thinking of a definite place, a place where I see evil and try to overcome it. To talk about it is an invitation to be silent about ultimate causes. What we call evil is here, in this place, just as much as what we call good, intermingled in the daily life of our cultures, our choices, and our refusals. We feel that it is impossible to make a clear separation between good and evil. Just as when women mix ingredients for a soup or a pie, we clearly know good and evil to be inextricably present and commingled in our own bodies. With a delicacy of our own we balance on the edge of this abyss in which we live or, rather, in which we exist. My body is my good and my evil! My good and my evil together live in my body!

This immanence and transcendence of evil calls me to view God differently and even to speak differently of the good news. Talk that is not so absolute or so certain seems more suitable to these difficult times. Poetic language, which reveals and hides things at the same time, seems better fitted to heal our wounds and to help us search out, in this age of common tragedy, new ways to learn to live together.

The transcendence and immanence of evil calls me to be converted to the reality I observe, this mingled reality where no word can be complete, no God can be all-powerful, no good can be completely victorious, and no evil can have the last word over life. This somber experience of the transcendence and immanence of evil permeates my existence in everything I do. Might this be what our traditional theologians called "original sin"? If so, I live it in my bones.

CHAPTER 2

evil and gender

"One is not born a woman; one becomes it." This noted saying of Simone de Beauvoir leads us to suspect that there is no conformity between one's biological sex and one's gender. The distinction between sex and gender has been clarified in part through the efforts of feminism, with its analysis of gender as it relates to the social identities of men and women. De Beauvoir's reflection, no doubt influenced by the concept of human choice as developed in Jean-Paul Sartre's philosophy, makes us think about the situation of women. What does *become* actually mean? Can one really choose what to become in a culture where certain social roles are fixed like fate? Which women have the privilege of choosing? To what extent is it possible to change the historic constructions that have fashioned our culture or the cultural constructions that have fashioned our history? How can the concept of gender, used as an interpretive tool, help us understand evil, particularly the evil endured by women? In this chapter I will use these questions as a foundation to analyze the concept and role of gender in analyzing the problem of evil.

The Concept of Gender

What exactly does the term *gender* mean? Is it only the declaration of male and female in humanity? How shall we explain this word? And what is the goal of any reflection that uses gender as an interpretive tool in a theological and feminist approach to evil? For the sake of clarity in answering these questions, we need to confront history and theory in some precise way.

At the heart of feminism in the 1980s, analyses of gender have set a value on the sexes and denounced the use of power deriving from the differences between them.[1] Feminists consider gender to be an important tool in pointing out the inadequacy of various theories attempting to use biology to explain the societal inequality between women and men. A gender-based analysis reveals the powers that affect the social division of labor and those aspects of social life that affect relationships between men and women. Feminists are unanimous in saying that analyses using gender have helped us avoid two big dangers: one is holding up the male as normative for humanity (androcentrism), and the other is believing in the neutrality of scientific study.[2] The category of gender invites us to abandon a certain simplicity about theological knowledge and to construct a more inclusive theory of the Christian faith.

There has never been any unanimous feminist perspective on the role and power of difference. In fact, discussions focused on the opposition between men and women have not made much progress toward a new understanding. Without going directly into the conflicts among various theories, I would like to clarify my personal position on this subject, one close to that of Julia Kristeva and Joan Scott.[3] In my view, the difference of gender is one among many. There are differences between men and women, between men and men, between women and women, and these differences intersect with differences in age, culture, religion, and many other areas. Nonetheless, without absolutizing the concept of gender, I want to emphasize its importance for understanding the intricacy of human relations from a particular angle. It is a device for viewing transformations in social relationships, whether in the public or the private domain. This tool is also applicable to political analysis of the social relationships between men and women.

Using the concept of gender, women can understand at least partially, in spite of all their differences, what is happening to them. They take note that their relations with others are always marked by contradictions and antagonisms but that it is always necessary to try to gain a better understanding so as to change situations fraught with injustice. The concept of gender has become, particularly in the human sciences, not only a tool for analysis but a tool for building the female self and, starting with a respect for difference, attempting to build social relationships more deeply anchored in justice and equality.

The first aim of a reflection on gender is to illuminate a whole system of power relations based on the social, political, and religious roles of our reality as sexual beings and, more precisely, to show how relations between men and women function to maintain a certain social and religious order and how new relations can change it. I hope to show in this chapter how relations between the sexes have been a source of evil and how theology has reinforced prejudices already present in different cultures. While engaged in a discourse about equality in principle and theory, I hope to show how deeply theology has been complicit in accentuating the inferiority of women.

I start with the affirmation that gender is not just the biological fact of being a man or a woman: gender is a social construct, a way of being in the world—a way of being educated and also a way of being perceived—that conditions our existence and action. I will attempt to show that gender subordinates some people to others not only through social class but also through a sociocultural construct of relationships between women and men, between male and female.[4] Sexuality is enculturated in power relationships. Thanks to awareness of this sociocultural construct—gender—women who were silent are finding their voices; those who were marginalized by the broader social and political process are trying to find their place and gain a better grasp of their situation.

Reflection on gender makes us discover a political question that was not even suspected earlier. Further, it opens us to a theopolitical question, that is, to a question about historical consequences induced by theological discourse. This discourse is not neutral: it is influenced by historical realities, ideologies, power games in which it was born and interpreted.[5]

The question of the social construct of gender is not first and foremost an abstract theoretical question but something that can be observed in practical relationships. As a woman leader of a popular movement in Brazil has said: "When a woman is born, she is born with a tag: You are a woman. You are made for washing and ironing. And when a man is born they say: You are going to work and have power over women. So it is often difficult to work with men . . . and I think it is difficult for them too. They have been raised this way and they are accustomed to have power over others."[6] Without mentioning the word *gender*, this woman made an analysis using it. She demonstrated that cultures forecast social roles and that there are conflicts among these roles. She showed how biology under the influence of culture is a source of prejudice and injustice.

Gender affects not only the male and female but the elements that enter into these relations, elements that take biological sex for granted but go beyond it. To speak of gender means, among other things, to speak of a certain way of being in the world based, on the one hand, on the biological character of our being and, on the other, on a character beyond biology because it is a fact of culture, history, society, ideology, and religion. In this sense, to speak of gender is to speak in the plural, given the differences in our culture and situation. Likewise, to declare gender is to declare the plurality of the human person.

The biological human being is a biological enculturated being, a biological entity that does not exist independent of the reality—social, communitarian, "other"—in which each person lives. There is no way to isolate the biological human being and to describe it as a given, independent of the totality of the human reality. Thus to speak of gender is not the same thing as to name the sex. Questions bearing on gender are much more encompassing than those related to the genitals of an individual, even if it seems at first glance that genitals are the determining factor. Hence the importance of this hermeneutical concept of gender in any consideration of human history.

Studies on the question of evil from the perspective of gender are few, especially in theology. European and Latin American literature is still deficient on this subject. Most existing analyses on the question of evil do not use gender as an interpretive category. North American women authors, however, have made significant and interesting advances in this area.[7] In my own enterprise I will use the concept of gender as an instrument to gain a better understanding of women's experience of evil. Its limits will be determined more or less by a social theory of gender.[8] But using this concept to analyze the life of witnesses from literature and to make a theological contribution to the subject derives from my own personal experience. Given the goal of my research, I place the greatest importance on the actual experience of women and their own words. And this experience shows that evil presents itself to women with a special face.

The concept of gender will appear as an addition to the problem of evil. It will expand our understanding of evil as it discloses its own complexity. By beginning with gender one sees evil differently, just as when one begins with social class. What is bad for the worker is not the same thing as what is bad for the employer even if, for instance, they both suffer from the same physical malady. One suffers it in easy circumstances and the other in indigence. The same disease is an evil for them both, but each endures it in his or her own condition. These conditions—economic, social, cultural, biological, psychological—mark the way in which each person undergoes evil and speaks of it. From this perspective the concept of gender opens up new horizons. We can now acknowledge not only the fact that humanity is composed of men and women with their own roles but also the fact that our way of organizing the world, of expressing ourselves, of thinking, believing, and articulating our deepest convictions is permeated by this fundamental biocultural reality that constitutes our being. It is here, at this underlying level, that one can grasp the presence of evil.

The question of gender exposes what has long been hidden: that this constitutive reality of the human being is also a historical construct in which evil manifests itself in a special way. This fundamental reality is indeed marked by the mystery of evil, by a laceration in the human being, by the domination and exclusion we experience in our relations. But it introduces further something special and new in our understanding of the human being, of God, and of the Christian faith. It reveals an aspect hitherto hidden and reveals it today through new means. Specifically it invites us to revisit our theoretical constructs about God and to examine cultural and social implications in the life of women and men in a given context.

Thus gender is not some supplementary theme offered to theological reflection, but a significant correction brought to bear on the anthropological and epistemological structure of theological thought. The concept of gender shows that, even if women and men of the same culture have similar perceptions, they have differences, particularly in their roles and expectations, the organization and division of work, and the expression of feelings proper to the expectations of each social group.

Here I will dwell more on the question of evil and show how it is permeated by the question of gender in a special way. No doubt there exists an intersection, a crossing of data that demonstrate still more neatly the complexity of human evil. We must be attentive to this intersection of data so as not to fall into a new absolutizing. Gender is a key to understanding certain aspects of human relations, but it is not a perfect key. Nonetheless, using gender as a lens adds specific value to an analysis. Listing some aspects of this particular tool will help us better understand its usefulness.

The Relativity of Difference

Gender enables us to do away with the universalism of male discourse about evil and allows us to enter into the relativity of difference. This relativity discloses not only the originality of each experience but something more profound: in my opinion it reveals the fact that the victims not only are the weak, the marginalized of society, but belong to the other sex. What constitutes humanity— the creative difference between the sexes—is one of the special locations in which evil demonstrates its work. But who established the division between the genders in their many historical expressions? Why have these men and women who need one another established a hierarchy based on their bodies and started a kind of war in their relationships?[9] And why does this relation between bodies, the site of good and evil, become, especially for women, a place of crucifixion and a place of exclusion?

Analyses using gender broaden our conception of masculine versus feminine by showing that we must go beyond a social hierarchical construct, binary and absolute, in which one term is always inferior to the other. Gender gives us one more key to understand the dynamics of social injustices, especially those that are grounded in the relation between men and women and particularly in theological formulations. These analyses open up to us a different view on the symbolism of evil to the extent that one introduces a dynamic in human relations going beyond mere opposition. Gender calls us to go beyond those fixed models that, for example, oppose Eve to Mary and present them as two contradictory exemplars. The concept of gender exposes the complexity of these symbolic models and leads us to decipher them in the light of social power games between men and women. In this way we can see how culture and politics fabricate gender and how gender builds culture and politics.

Gender as a Hermeneutical Tool

We do well to remember that gender directs us beyond our sex, which is a biological factor not chosen, something we are subject to that situates us in a social or sociobiological construct. When children are born, each infant finds itself awaited in a certain way, welcomed differently as a boy or as a girl. There is a culture in biology and a biology in culture in which oppositions, ways of being, and values are already present.

To say *gender* is to say male and female in their relation to social and cultural output, in the creation and learning of behavior, and in the reproduction of those same behaviors. To say *man* or *woman* is already to introduce a certain way of existing in the world, proper to each sex, a way of being the product of a complex web of cultural relationships. *Female* and *male* also have their effect on relationships between women and men exercised in private and in public. The notion of gender, bigger than biological sex, incorporates this relationship dynamic.

The sociologist Pierre Bourdieu, in his ethnological study of the Kabyles, supports the suspicions of feminists in their analyses of male texts. As he sees it, distinct identities are established as habits through an immense and continuous work of socialization. A game of opposition, verified in every culture, occurs between what is attributed symbolically to men and what is attributed symbolically to women. It leads us to perceive the world according to the principles of the dominant social structure, that is, that this structure seems to be something natural, something that has always operated that way. Based on a social construction of sex, or more precisely on a social definition of sexual identity, this structure is equally responsible for the way the behaviors for each sex are rigidly fixed.[10]

The dominant social and cultural structure also reveals how deeply a cult of virility, which is based on the primacy of masculinity and those qualities attributed to the masculine, is embedded in our societies. This notion enters into the culture and our subconscious and grows. In discourse and analysis, says Bourdieu, the male vision of the world is presented as evidence and functions as an ideology justifying what exists. In order to understand the male domination and the female submission present in our symbolic world, it is not enough merely to bring critical knowledge to bear. We have to take notice of things over which knowledge has no control. It often happens that we have knowledge of what oppresses us but we do not have the means to change the rules of the game of oppression. Knowledge is certainly important in the process of transformation, but it is not enough to bring about actual change. To change the very conditions that produce relationships of domination, there must be a collective process of education. There must be agreement, a minimal consensus, a common analysis to intercept what has become habitual. As Bourdieu says, there must be a change in the symbolic order and then a change in actual practice, in the daily life of the culture.

The domain of theology is particularly the domain of the symbolic production of meaning and a special place for reproducing the dominant social and cultural structure. We know how widely the symbolic world of Christianity, and particularly of published theology, is dominated by male symbols. From this point of view, theology in all its aspects becomes a privileged place of action in view of a revolution in symbolism. Thus feminist theologians work to deconstruct patriarchal theology and to build a more inclusive theology. The weight of cultural mores is beginning slowly to be weakened by feminist theories and particularly by analyses based on gender.

Using gender as a hermeneutical tool is not without controversy among feminists.[11] As I mentioned above, it is not my purpose to enter into a discussion of this controversy, but I would like to recall several points of critique that place my reflections in context and define their parameters. Recall that by beginning with the concept of gender, French and North American feminists want to use sexuality in the same way that Marxists use the notion of work. Workers experience estrangement from their work through the exploitation of their work by bosses or by the dominant class. Similarly, women experience estrangement from their sexuality through the exploitation of their sexuality and theft of their autonomy by male domination.[12]

In Marxism the concept of social class has become a universal concept, capable of explaining the dynamic of history. Likewise, for certain feminists the category of gender has become almost a new universal, capable of explaining in great measure the origin of domination suffered by women.

For my part, I want to emphasize the importance of the category of gender as an interpretive tool that opens new possibilities for analysis, at the same time saying "no" to universalizing gender as the only category and one that takes in the experience of all women. Likewise, I distance myself from identification of women as a social class, as in Marxist analysis in which workers are a social class opposed to owners. Women are socially located, but they are not a class against the class of men. Concretely, if I adopt experience as the point from which to begin my reflection, I rediscover specific identities of women, individual stories, personal sentiments, and definite struggles. I discover, first of all, lives of women with a name and a history; I hear their cries of sorrow in their situations. I discover, too, happy or unhappy relationships between men and women. The category of gender helps me perceive the dynamic of relations and power, but it cannot be considered as a new, unblemished concept or one that explains all oppression of women. If we reject the fetishism of virility, we cannot establish gender as a new fetish. If we reject totalitarian discourse, we cannot establish a key concept to explain everything. We must always maintain the dialectic of male–female relations, understanding that human life unfolds in continual interaction between the two sexes.

Another important aspect of feminist theory present in analysis based on gender is the way the theorists' explanations construct utopias. While freeing ourselves to make a critique about the oppression or submission of women, we are trying to present an emancipating utopia. But there are many kinds of utopias. One is a world more self-contained for women, and another would open new forms of relations between men and women. It is clear that each of these utopias has its limits. But we must admit that there is no way to present alternative thought and action without sketching out a utopia, the outline of a salvation, provisory and limited though it may be. I myself envision a utopia of humanity, men and women together trying to build better relations of justice and solidarity.

The utopia sketched out in this reflection is a utopia for women, but not a monopoly. It is a utopia of sharing, of mutual recognition of men's and women's values. It incorporates a plurality of discourse deriving from a plurality of cultures and people. Finally, it is a utopia tied to the experience of the life of Jesus of Nazareth and to a whole tradition that has wanted to safeguard its wisdom and its struggle for justice, respect, and equality among people.

Gender and Epistemology

Before examining the implications of connecting gender and the experience of evil, I want to recall how urgently this question pushes us to re-envisage our scientific knowledge. In this regard let me mention some significant points concerning epistemology, specifically, an epistemology of evil—a way of telling it, knowing it, trying to denounce it, and also fighting it. What is new, as I see it, is this: the very epistemology that reveals evil and denounces it can also produce it by obscuring certain aspects of human reality. It can thus generate exclusionary processes that themselves generate evil. Recently, thanks to the development of feminist epistemologies, we have been taking note of the limited and extremely androcentric nature of modern science.[13] Feminism denounces any knowledge considered scientific that results in excluding women and the marginalized. When we introduce gender into epistemology, a different way of understanding human knowledge emerges. And this new way affects all our knowledge by starting from a perspective that disorients us and that invites us to change our traditional points of reference.

Critiquing the Universalism of Social Science

A consideration of gender brings us to a critique of social science. In other words, various social sciences, like philosophy, psychology, and theology, have made proclamations on different subjects and presented them as "human," when in reality they refer to male experience and, further, to experience in the Western world. "Universal theory" is actually male theory; it is centralized in the places of dominant power and in social relations allied to power. Abundant examples are found everywhere, but especially in theology.

It is sufficient, for example, to look at the Bible to see how our eyes have been and still are more attentive to men's action than to women's. While affirming that God is Spirit, we note that our relationship to this mystery is masculine, and those who represent it in history are men.[14] Further, we speak of the tradition of the fathers of the church as if the community of believers can dispense with the presence of mothers of the church. Today the role of women in building the church seems entirely superfluous.

We speak of the disciples, apostles, and followers as if they were all men and as if the establishing of the church could have taken place without the devout action of thousands of women. The claim is made that what we know is historical because documents attest to it. We are dealing with a social science limited to documents, compiled by men and recognized as official, but no one even suspects that another history might have been written.[15] The silence or hiddenness of women in actions called public reflects the privilege of male agents and their centrality in history. It reveals also a ladder of values, a hierarchy established according to what culture considers superior and inferior.

One might object, as indeed some do, that in language the masculine includes the feminine, but this means that language itself reveals the established norm. Here we confront one inclusion that hides the other. It is now necessary to stress an inclusion that will reveal the other, that will unveil it and make it appear in its own original form and with proper dignity.

We discover the same arrangement in the development of historical knowledge as well as in the contemporary behavior of most people. This male-centeredness present in our culture influences our knowledge. We can say that the most noted traits of Western theological epistemology are male-oriented; that is, the affirmations said to be scientific, and even those of faith, refer to what men have observed and to the creation of a universal masculine discourse. An epistemology that takes account of the feminine will criticize the identification of what men perceive as universal perception. It will uncover the character of the perspectives that influence our knowledge, marked also by relationships of gender. These relationships are limited and always in motion. This does not mean that there are no similarities or agreement on many topics. But we are concerned in this reflection with introducing the notion of gender as one source of the relativity of knowledge and as one means of making what has been hidden come to light.

Overcoming Dualism

The question of gender leads us to overcome dualism, a way of thinking permanently rooted in Western scholarship. Dualism manifests itself in the form of opposition, affirming the negativity or the lesser value of one pole relative to the other. Such dualism is not only epistemological but also ethical. A clear-cut division between good and evil, as well as a narrow, precise judgment about what is good, has sharpened this dualism. The feminine side has always been considered dark, inferior, less gifted, or closer to the material world. The masculine side has been judged superior, bright, and closer to the spiritual, more suitable for representing God. Thus we see the close connection between epistemological questions, ethical questions, and questions of gender.

All epistemology can be seen as ethics, and all ethics is epistemology. Knowledge that scorns the contribution of women is not only limited and partial; it is an exclusionary knowledge. The fact that it claims to be universal already shows its limits. We can say that at the concrete level of feminist analysis such knowledge is not attentive to the ethical dimension of justice, equality, and respect for the plurality of beings and their experience. It reduces the other to oneself and does not even ask whether the contribution of others who are different is important. While this statement about traditional epistemology expresses something of the past, it is still

boldly present and is a kind of judgment aimed at more just relationships. Justice is set forth as a reciprocity and respect between
the male and female sides of humanity. Respect for difference is an
ethical and epistemological element.

Nevertheless, one might fear that respect for difference leads to
ethical relativism or laissez-faire in the matter of human relations.
Feminist ethics is alert to these traps. We are always aware that the
risk of demeaning the human person is present everywhere. Respect
for differences carries that risk just as much as the idealistic and
sometimes dogmatic universalism of Western ethics. All models
of behavior harbor risks of degradation, extremism, or exclusion.
But this argument about the danger of relativism cannot stand up
in the face of the actual challenges of our history. Our knowledge
is always relative to historical context, to cultural conditions, to
ideologies. Today the challenges that call us to rethink epistemology come from the intermingling of cultures—indeed, the globalization of cultures—imposed by a world economy, new means
of communication, and the awakening of the consciousness of
women striving to be recognized as subjects in all of history.

The feminist epistemological question also touches on theological epistemology. While it is not the particular subject of this
reflection, it is necessary at least to point out its importance and to
mention its rudiments. Claiming that the concept of gender
enables us to do away with epistemological dualisms means doing
away with a discontinuity often present in Christian theology
between the things of God and the things of human beings.
When we speak in these terms, it is as if, in our most inner
thoughts, a chasm opens unveiling the contradictions present in
our speech. This chasm is not just symbolic language to indicate
the presence of the mystery that lies beyond us. It has been prop-
agated as reality, the reality of our world and of our faith, the
expression of what is referred to as the world of God and the
world of human beings.

This epistemological schema, besides being dualistic, is also sexist and human-centered. To say that it is sexist means it values one

sex over the other. To say that it is human-centered means that all
of nonhuman nature is practically forgotten or considered merely
as an object to serve human beings. From this perspective the centrality of the male is always present, given that it is men who say
this and who place themselves in the most eminent side of humanity. Furthermore, there are activities and values considered male
that seem to be the most appreciated and most influential in
human relations. The male affirms God to be totally Other, but an
Other who is revealed in history to have a male face.

The tool of gender makes suspect the experiential reality of this
schema and also denounces maintaining injustice against women
at the level of consciousness. When we speak of experiential reality we mean simply acknowledging the difficulty of living concretely what is told us by theology. There is no lack of examples
to justify this statement. We need only recall the works of two
great theologians of the church, St. Augustine and St. Thomas
Aquinas.[16] Their theology is constructed from an anthropological
vision that holds woman to be a less perfect being, more disposed
to depravity. In parallel terms, what is said about God eliminates,
so it seems, any trace of the feminine.[17] This theological discourse
ultimately justifies men's power not only in civil society but in the
church as well.

Cultural Relativism: A Positive Aspect

The question of gender helps us discover in cultural relativism a
positive factor in the richness of the human being. Our knowledge
is made up of different perspectives and ideologies but also of different experiences according to whether we are male or female.
This fact demonstrates that a culture of gender or a cultural gender is more important than we might think. Gender here means a
reality of taboos, sanctions, expectations, ordinances, beliefs, and
impressions that play a role in the relationships between men and
women.

A hierarchical dualistic society, organized under the control of
men, favors one pole over the other, as I have said earlier. Norms of

behavior are created for both sexes, establishing patterns that can doubtless change but in the meantime not only replicate those behaviors but even affect the very structure of our personalities. Thus one becomes a woman according to the norms established by culture. This development is marked by our sociocultural heritage, marked too by that side of our existence that we did not choose and that encounters a harsher reality when it is, for example, the life of a poor woman in a third world country. In such a context important choices toward greater autonomy are often not at all possible. People live or survive as best they can. Speaking of cultural relativism from a feminist perspective means noting the fact that in general any analysis of the culture conforms to roles already predetermined. Awareness of the relative nature of these roles constitutes one of the most important contributions of feminism.

The feminist movement, especially in Latin America in its complexity and diversity, attempts to evoke the necessity of acting concretely on this social destiny—the predetermined roles for each gender—and through simple actions recovering dignity lost or obscured. The concept of gender gives us a glimpse of one in relation to another and helps us understand each self constructing itself. In feminist scholarship, gender exercises a critique of those generalizations about the "other" so characteristic of the modern era and our Western Christian ethic. It is no longer a matter of making formal statements about principles, rights, and the universal duties of individuals, important as that is. It is no longer a matter of making one-sided statements and calling them universal.

The mediation of gender calls for universality to become particular, for rights and duties to be applied to actual subjects in concrete situations. Indeed, what governs our relations with one another is actual reality and its most pressing needs according to the particular context. The dimension of otherness, a major concern of Emmanuel Levinas, is particularly enlightening. Fundamentally, the other is like me, but the other is also one who is different from me and who brings me up short by his or her difference. If I am not to reduce the other to myself, an ethical and epistemological effort must maintain the tension within the richness of difference created by the pluralism of concrete lived experience.[18]

Daily Routine in the Historiography of Women
Through the lens of gender, daily life appears as an important element in the historiography of women. Daily life—as opposed to grand historical facts, like wars, space exploration, or great scientific inventions—is the fight to live today, to look for work, to do the cooking, to bathe children and do laundry, to exchange the gestures of love, to find meaning in life. Daily life is the domestic world, the world of short-term relationships, more direct interactions capable of changing larger relationships. Incorporating women's daily life in that knowledge called universal means including the concrete, those things necessary for life or mere survival. Daily life is routine, the habitual, everyday activities of family, children, neighbors—everything that makes up the immediate fabric of our existence. Daily life includes our personal stories, the way we feel about events, our reactions as we read the papers or watch television; in short, our responses to reality. Into this milieu we are born, suffer, love, and die. The daily life of men and women as part of history shows that major economic and political enterprises affect how we live at home. Domestic life is not divorced from big socioeconomic stakes or the great challenges of culture. It forms part of larger economic and cultural structures because they exist concretely at this regional, interpersonal, communitarian level.[19]

With this appreciation of daily life we develop a different conception of time. Time is lived out in our daily duties, spontaneous gestures, relations of friendship, personal limits, likes and dislikes, choice of food, looking at ourselves in a mirror, conversations over a good cup of coffee. Daily life, and especially that of women, is a place where history is made and where different forms of oppression and of unacknowledged evil show up. No doubt these were always present, but our eyes could not see them. What has been hidden now appears, thanks to feminism and particularly to the development of the concept of gender. A certain prophetic quality enriches our efforts to recover the lives of our mothers and fore-bears and our own lives as important sites in the unfolding of history. And these sites, typically considered unimportant, become crucial in understanding why our lives have become cursed, why we are the bearers of a strain of human evil that makes its irrationality all the more incomprehensible.

Gender, Difference, and Violence

The preceding point opens a window on the role of gender for a better understanding of the problem of evil. I want to investigate the relationship among gender, difference, and violence against women. What is the meaning of difference in human beings? Of what difference are we speaking? Why emphasize it, especially in a time of such great divisions in human history?

That women are daily victims of a particular kind of violence is a common fact. Our bodies are fair game in wars, objects to be used in streets and concentration camps, always under threat from lustful looks inside and outside our homes. Domestic violence, which we cannot ignore, is growing alarmingly fast. The female body is an object above all others. Because it is perceived as an object, some think that women themselves must wish to be regarded that way. Many women behave like objects because deep down they believe in their existential inferiority, an inferiority legitimized by the culture. And so domination moves ahead with the complicity or at least the acquiescence of social structures. One of the questions that arises in this sad picture is an attempt to find out why the female body has become the target of violent desires, of vengeance, possession, conquest, exclusion. What is the weak point that attracts and triggers violence against women? What is in us that incites violence against ourselves? Even if I am unable to find the answer to these questions, just articulating this problem once more is an important step in our reflection.

I will open the debate on the question of difference with some ideas of René Girard. Can we speak of the difference between women and men in the same way we speak of the difference between cultures, religions, and races? What is the difference in this difference? In his work *The Scapegoat* Girard analyzes stereotypes of persecution:

> No culture exists within which everyone does not feel "different" from others and does not consider such "differences" legitimate and necessary. Far from being radical and progressive, the current glorification of difference is merely the abstract expression of an outlook common to all cultures. There exists in every individual a tendency to think of himself not only as different from others but as extremely different, because every culture entertains this feeling of difference among the individuals who compose it.[20]

When we speak of difference in gender or the social construct of gender, are we using this same interpretation of difference? Girard is surely right about specific cultural groups, but I believe that the question of women in their larger social relationships presents itself differently. Women are a constituent part of social life and as such dependent on cultural processes in which difference plays an important role in establishing social identity.

From a cultural or ethnological point of view, women are an integral part of society. They are inside one system even if they have distinct roles within it. But through the lens of gender the difference experienced by women in any culture is not based solely on the way other differences exist as identified by sociologists and anthropologists. Likewise, the difference is not primarily, as essentialist philosophers like Plato would have it, based on assigning a kind of essence proper to women just as they might assign an essence proper to men. But from the phenomenological perspective of gender, the difference is a historical process that has subjected women to domination and marginalization because of their enculturated biology. Thus we can say that this biologically enculturated difference has in its own way generated a social and political differentiation as well as forms of domination and support for a male-defined social and sexual hierarchy.

This institutionalized differentiation has forced women to take on certain burdens and behaviors as if these were part of their biological destiny. Discussion of difference has justified inequality, especially when it is presented as legitimated by the laws of nature or the will of the gods. From a feminist perspective, affirming difference can be also the acceptance of a state of unjust relationships ending in violence. Some ways of thinking about difference accentuate the domination and exclusion of women. Respect for difference does not give any ideological justification for favoring some to the detriment of others, as happened in the justification of slavery.

In *Violence and the Sacred* Girard insists that the desire to imitate is the basis for violence. Can we say this about women? How do we explain mimicking as a cause of inequality between men and women? Who is imitating whom? Can we say that it is because of envy or a desire to imitate that women are violated, that their bodies are used to maintain a system of exclusion?

> The mimetic quality of childhood desire is universally recognized. Adult desire is virtually identical, except that (most strikingly in our own culture) the adult is generally ashamed to imitate others for fear of revealing his lack of being. The adult likes to assert his independence and to offer himself as a model to others; he invariably falls back on the formula, "Imitate me!" in order to conceal his own lack of originality.
>
> Two desires converging on the same object are bound to clash. Thus, mimesis coupled with desire leads automatically to conflict.[21]

But what is the actual meaning of this "imitation" when it comes to relations between men and women? And how can we understand imitation at the heart of the violence based on gender when the other, who seems to be the object of desire, is diminished, violated, almost wiped out? The conflict almost always ends in silence, the destruction or suppressing of the other. How explain systemic violence against women, not only in a specific situation like war, rape, and the prostitution of young girls? How explain institutionalized violence, subtle and disguised?

Institutionalized violence against women is not just one specific act of violence but a social arrangement, a cultural construct geared to degrade one pole of humanity and exalt another. We are only at the level of observation and not of research into causes that offer an explanation. All the theories that attempt to sketch out a possible explanation turn out to be incomplete. Even if I pose here indirectly the question of causality, I am persuaded that the path to follow is to seek personal and institutional honesty rooted in the here and now. Such honesty involves recognizing that there is a sickness in our social relationships and that we are all, men and women alike, victims of its contagion and spreaders of this same disease. In the face of this sin that touches us all insofar as we are human, it is necessary to find ways to escape it, to find some paths to a possible salvation.

What is the advantage for the violent man? What advantage or profit does he gain from the object he violates? Should we at this point introduce Girard's reflection on the role of the rival? For Girard the rival is the model for the subject on the basis of desire. In terms of male–female relationships I wonder whether the rival should be another man. In reality, rivalry is between men, perhaps over a woman—or is there such a thing as men's rivalry against women? No doubt we need to go more deeply into this investigation at an anthropological as well as a psychological level. Rivalry from the viewpoint of an enculturated biology might be an interesting factor, even if I do not have the opportunity of pursuing it here. It makes me think of Freud in his analysis of what girls want. He says that girls have penis envy. And do boys have desires for what girls can do—bear children and breast-feed? Would these desires be a source of violence for men?

In our life and our culture today, we see that women are objects of desire for men; women are also treated as men's property. But they are objects of desire because of men's desire for ownership and pleasure, not out of men's desire to be women. Can we say that when violence is used against women, it is really against the hierarchical structure of society? Can we say that a woman's body is a body used for revenge or to express a larger rebellion? Why this violence against the innocent?

The Christian version of violence experienced by the innocent does not justify violence. Still, violence experienced by the innocent has often served as an excuse for continuing and justifying violent procedures. We must not forget how sacrificial love, especially of the innocent, and passive acceptance of suffering and humility are qualities idealized in Jesus. This idealization reinforces, as Mary Daly says, the scapegoat syndrome in women.[22] Girard's theory, in spite of its value, is open to critique from the perspective of feminists or of oppressed people. The originality of his thought is seriously limited if one takes another approach.[23] Might there be another way to understand this irrationality or this violence that marks our relationships? These questions have led me to analyze the relation between nature and culture as a further step in understanding the enigma of evil as women experience it.

Nature and Culture

Thinking about the relationship between nature and culture is another important aspect of feminist reflection on the devaluation of women. Further, exploring this field of research will help us to improve not only our understanding of the question of hierarchy in anthropology, which is at the basis of Catholic theology, but our interpretation of the evil women experience.

The identification of women with nature (or likening nature to a woman) is nothing new. In various cultures it is popular to speak of nature as a mother who nourishes her children. Indigenous people of the Americas have always spoken of Mother Earth as a divinity who gives life.[24] But if one associates nature with a maternal image, one summons up at the same time the image of an uncontrollable reality, violent, savage, capable of bringing disorder. These two views have been identified with the female sex and can be found in several ancient cultures.[25] Nevertheless it is the second image that seems to have served the scientific revolution in its determination to conquer nonhuman nature. From this image comes the idea of power over nature and, indirectly from the same symbolism, power over women.

Women have been symbolically considered to be closer to nature because of their role in birth, lactation, and care of newborns. Men have been regarded as creators of culture because of their activity in hunting, fishing, and war. It is important to recognize that, from a patriarchal point of view, making artifacts, cooking, preparing medicinal herbs, and knowing how to clean and sew are not considered works of culture but something inferior. In this work I will not be going deeply into questions of cultural anthropology and ethnology, but it does seem important to mention them in order to broaden our consideration. Similarly the idea of (nonhuman) nature as a living organism to which one owes respect and obedience has lost ground progressively in the course of history, even if occasionally there remain traces of fertility cults and earth worship. The earth has become a source of profit, a place for commercial exploitation. A dualist approach can be found even in men and women who want to avoid it. We see nature as the opposite of humans, as if human beings were not part of nature, of all living beings, of the ecosystem. And we set them in opposition particularly to mark the superiority and power of humans, especially men.

This kind of dualism or separation between humans and nature is growing greater and greater. And in this process of accentuating the separation, woman's body remains a place of conflict while man's body (the body of reason) has become capable not only of freeing itself from nature but also of dominating nature through science and technology. The mechanical understanding of the laws of nature and of life, so broadly disseminated in the time of Isaac Newton and René Descartes, gives legitimacy to manipulating nature. At the same time it reduces the contribution of women to the sphere of home and children, the least important of all spheres, even though it is fundamental for continuing human society. The symbolic proximity of women to physical nonhuman nature has surely contributed to the predominance of culture over nature. Nature, it would seem, becomes more beautiful and necessary in the measure to which culture intervenes, that is, in the measure to which a man's mind transforms it for his own use. From that point on, nature and women's bodies are defined by men and controlled by men, their masters. This definition illumines men's public discourse on nature and women and at the same time explains women's public silence about themselves.

Since the European Renaissance, women have been objectified in their connection with nature, whether put on a pedestal by artists or persecuted as witches by the Inquisition. In the first instance, artists portrayed women as close to nature, or likened nature to women. Countless pieces of Renaissance art link the beauty of nature with the beauty of the female body. In the second, witches were the symbol of nature gone awry, needing to be controlled to stop its crimes. The cultural prejudice that attributed evil inclinations to women's character launched the hunt for witches, individuals who were actually gifted women seeking autonomy in their lives.[26] This ideological relation between women and nature, and especially between rebellious nature and women, has reinforced prejudice against women and contributed to a process of oppression and exclusion, which is also found in theology.

In Western culture, nonhuman nature is linked to women as something simultaneously natural and cultural. This connection appears in sexual tourism and language used about young girls as virgin forests, ready to be conquered by men. Making this kind of comparison accentuates dualisms and increases social injustices. The same kind of theme can be found in Christian theology. Note how, in the official documents of the Catholic church, for example, there is talk of woman's vocation of motherhood but rarely any mention of man's vocation of fatherhood.[27] Similarly, in the allotting of guilt and punishment related to sexuality and reproduction, a much heavier burden is placed on women than on men.

In spite of the official pronouncements of the church concerning women, some theologians exhibit a certain goodwill about lifting up the feminine as well as the masculine in humanity.[28] But although woman and the qualities we call feminine may be exalted, still people forget actual women, their tears, and the complicity that has produced destructive behaviors. This appeal to the concrete dimension of existence lies at the heart of feminism's attempt to think of human and nonhuman nature beyond simplistic oppositions or ideologies of power. A new symbolism is needed to do justice to that vital web of interdependence in which we exist.

Gender and Women's Experience of Evil

How shall we express more precisely the question of gender in connection with women's experience of evil? What are the actual insights introduced by this new interpretive tool? What changes in discourse about evil affect theology? Evil endured by women is undoubtedly linked to the fact that they are considered a second sex, not only different but of lesser value. Second means not just different but inferior, according to our culture as well as our philosophies and theologies. The concept of gender has helped us see not only conflicts of power between the sexes but a division in domains, a different conception of time, a different understanding of the relation between nature and culture, a different practical ethic, and values lived out differently.

In the light of this interpretive concept, the witness of women's lives, as we have seen, shows us how much the domestic scene is not only full of dreams of happiness but also a special source of unhappiness for women. This home base, large or small, is shaped by oppressive relationships, which derive from harmful economic, political, and social structures as well as cultural prejudices. But a woman's domestic experience is also directly affected by the very fact that she is a woman.

Sacrifice in the Life of Women

In this stage of my reflection I will develop two points I see as important to some aspects of Christian theology, the issues of self-sacrifice and guilt. Neither has received much attention in Latin American feminist theology, although significant efforts are under way. In bringing up these questions I will try to open new theological windows so as to rethink the complexity of evil, trying to go beyond a narrative phenomenology of evil as women see it. I am not forgetting my witnesses: they inspired this approach, even though I am not now making a direct appeal to their experience and words.

In the Christian tradition sacrificing one's life for others is often considered in a positive light. Sacrificing oneself for the good of another is an act that at first glance deserves praise. Voluntary self-sacrifice for another's benefit is linked to liberty, to a personal choice of certain values in life. This kind of sacrifice will always keep its positive aspect, whether in philosophical humanism or as a religious choice or, quite simply, in relationships between family members or friends. It is not the positive character of sacrifice I want to discuss, however, but instead how it is used to reinforce those in power, those who possess the power to manipulate people's lives for the good of a few.

We know that religion and even culture use self-sacrifice as a means to maintain a certain power over individuals. This behavior is almost as old as humanity. Sacrifice in its different forms has always been used as a kind of barter or exchange to obtain things from gods and goddesses or from people. In the same way, economic systems make people sacrifice themselves for profit or for some other promised gain. In daily conversation it is common to hear: "This was obtained through heavy sacrifice" or "One must make sacrifices to succeed" or "Without sacrifice we will never succeed in creating social welfare." The need for sacrifice is always present, and this need is, for some people, a daily burden in keeping themselves alive. To live or just to survive becomes a sacrifice that is a terrible tragedy and injustice. In such a case, sacrifice is a need that goes beyond the daily effort to do this or that. This kind of sacrifice demands that one's whole personality be engaged in an act without any assurance of arriving at the hoped-for end. It demands something surpassing what is considered normal for an ordinary life.

Here I do not want to go into an analysis of sacrifice in society, especially in our economic and neoliberal culture. I would rather examine how the sacrificial attitude in society, which probably copies religious ones, is an important support for maintaining the privileges of a minority and the afflictions of the majority. Through sacrifice one is promised paradise; if we make sacrifices, our happiness will come more quickly; if we make sacrifices, we can have a fine car or become beautiful women like Hollywood stars. Sacrifice is the means whereby we can enter into the heaven enjoyed by those of privilege. Here I want to ask: How is the question of gender related to sacrifice? To what degree is it present in the Christian tradition, which has fashioned so many cultures for two thousand years?

Using gender as a lens, we can interpret sacrifice as an element in theological constructs. For example, Christian tradition has emphasized the centrality of sacrifice as spiritual power and a means of salvation. Jesus Christ redeems us through his suffering, by the gift of his life. This purchase validates our own suffering and sacrifice. The sacrifice of Jesus Christ has been used to legitimate and justify the sacrifices of the Christian community. In the Pauline tradition certain spiritual themes stress the fact that our suffering adds to that of Christ. This spiritual path, we know, has had sad consequences in the lives of persons and communities. Today new theological currents, especially feminist ones, attempt to dislodge sacrifice from the central role it holds. Feminist theology advances a new path of salvation for women and also for the marginalized of history, for women and men who have to bear on their shoulders a far too heavy burden of suffering and scorn.

In this understanding we emphasize that the center of the life of Jesus was not sacrifice or suffering but works of justice, the arrival of relationships of mercy and solidarity. The core of Jesus' life was the battle against evil in all its manifestations. Over the years the emphasis has changed: the basis for understanding Jesus' role has shifted from the arrival of justice in history to sacrifice in view of eternal salvation. This theory has reinforced the value of dependence, sorrow, suffering, and martyrdom.

If this interpretation of Christianity has affected men and women, it has affected them differently. Given the patriarchal character of our society, the notion of sacrifice as good has a more powerful effect on those on the lower rungs of the social ladder. These are people in poverty and women, who by reason of their perceived inferiority have to make the greatest sacrifice and who have to make greater efforts to gain their salvation. It is women who identify most with the sacrifice of Jesus on the cross. He validates their suffering and gives meaning to their lives.

There is a hierarchy in sacrifice and a greater or lesser recognition of its value, depending on whether it is the sacrifice of the rich or the poor, of white or black, of man or woman. Sacrifices, even in religion, participate in the same hierarchical dualism present in society. One might point out that sometimes women receive less harsh sentences than men for the same crimes. When that happens, it is not because of special consideration for women but because of public recognition of lesser responsibility and the "dangerous nature" of women or perhaps a certain scorn for them. The theory of sacrifice has succeeded in encouraging in many women a kind of pleasure in suffering or even confusion between pleasure and sacrifice. Sacrifice and doing one's duty become a kind of enjoyment.

From a religious point of view, living in sacrifice is living in obedience to the will of the Father. And living in obedience to the Father means living in obedience to his Son, represented by father, husband, brothers, and men who hold social and religious power. The ideology of sacrifice, imposed by patriarchal culture, has developed in women a training in renunciation. They must give up their pleasure, thoughts, dreams, and desires in order to put themselves at the service of others or to live as others think they should. Women in many ways are made to serve others. At best they must accept sorrow and suffering to make the scraps of pleasure acceptable. In Latin America women who do not live according to this logic are called "easy." They threaten the established order and arouse fear and envy in those submissive to the law of duty and sacrifice.

Within the notion of sacrifice is the concept of a ransom: you have to pay a ransom in order to have what you want. This idea of paying a ransom occurs not only in the religious world but in cultural institutions that subtly promote sacrifice, whether to solicit donations or to control people's lives. Note how the market imposes sacrifices not only on the poor but especially on women by promoting the model of "being a woman." To achieve this model state, one needs to suffer. But one never reaches the ideal proposed, the ideal of a beautiful body or a perfect face. Gymnasiums and beauty parlors, new sanctuaries for the model body, are multiplying in poor countries. The password is "sacrifice," sacrifice to get what one knows one will never attain. Sacrifice is the key to the happiness of living in accordance with the norms established by the new global culture. Happiness or pleasure, even when it is limited, becomes an eschatological reality at the end of time. One must always wait without ever attaining. Pleasure is only something imaginary; one is beguiled by every kind of promise through every means of communication, including religious sermons, to attempt to reach it but one never actually attains it.

The ideology of sacrifice induces fear—fear of being separated from or abandoned by God; fear, too, of not being able to live up to the ideal deportment demanded by the culture; fear of not being accepted by men and recognized by other women. Fear of others leads inevitably to alienation from oneself. One does not become one's own person but what others expect. One loses a sense of self, often without even knowing it, and one conforms to the established models as if there were only one way of following our unique life and way to salvation. It is astonishing to hear women from Latin America and Africa say that in their countries women are brought up primarily "for men."[29]

Often we hear women, when they are undergoing some violent experience like sexual abuse, ask, "Why has God abandoned me?" They think they have been deserted by or separated from God because of their suffering. This attitude leads most women to endure and accept suffering as if it were part of God's design. The memory of Jesus' unjust suffering comes to mind and plays an ambiguous role. If it does sometimes motivate courage and love, it can also lead to masochism and alienation. It is still common to hear women in great trouble say, "Jesus suffered more than this." The suffering of another person, of a God-man, seems to be a way of accepting this (my) suffering and developing a certain conformity.

Enduring suffering imposed by the cross has been developed by religious traditions and social-religious systems as a veil to cover up different kinds of misery or unjust crosses. This veil does not allow us to distinguish between suffering caused by the wrongdoing of others and that existential anguish present in every human life.

I am persuaded that this unjust situation demands not only economic, social, and cultural reform but also a theological revision radically transforming the image of God as one who demands suffering as the price of happiness and exacts self-denial, with no attention to life's sources of pleasure. Feminist theology opens a path to a human vocation to pleasure, beauty, and largesse. Averse to saying that only one way of salvation exists for women and for humanity, feminist theology enters into the pluralistic dialogue of our times to influence its understanding of human relations. Within this multifold view feminist theology employs the concept of gender to reflect on personal and collective guilt.

Personal and Collective Guilt of Women

Thinking about sacrifice leads us to thinking about the guilt women feel. This feeling of guilt is not clearly defined, mainly because this thing one feels and names guilt is somewhat vague in the lives of women. It is an existential guilt with religious overtones, a feeling, a profound experience of a personal burden, added like a surplus to certain events. It is a distance between me and myself, a wound deep inside, an inconsistency between what I am and what I would like to be, a discord between the image I have of myself and what corresponds to societal or family expectations.[30] A kind of expected punishment lives in me without my exactly knowing why. What is the basis for this guilt? Where does it come from? What does it mean, and what are its consequences in the actual lives of women? Does this guilt have any connection with something the individual has done, or is it something in the way women are brought up?

These questions lead to the analysis of Paul Ricoeur, who makes a distinction between being finite and being guilty.[31] He speaks about being human, although his main interest is with the Christian religious experience. Ricoeur understands guilt to be knowledge of the inauthenticity of the human being in the face of historic aberrations. For my part, I intend to stay in the realm of the particular, that is, the concrete experience of women and of women in concrete circumstances. I see this kind of guilt as being without personal responsibility, without consciousness of some bad deed done.

A kind of guilt is present in the culture, one that judges some more guilty than others because of their cultural or biological condition. Some education also produces guilt and then reproduces it. The concept of gender allows us to observe this kind of guilt, whether in anthropological thought or theological discourse. Guilt comes from the culture itself, something not chosen. For many women such enculturated guilt is, then, an evil.

Let us note, first of all, that we are not speaking of women "in general." There is no such entity in concrete history. What I am saying relies on the witnesses presented earlier in chapter 1. I realize that the word *guilt* is rarely used in my testimony and that of the women cited. But just because the word is not used does not mean that the sentiment is absent. On the contrary, I think guilt bears on the behavior of all these women, often silently. It lives deep inside even if the word *fault* or *guilt* does not often appear. Guilt is always present like an uninvited guest. When women talk about their lack of ownership and their access to knowledge, their lack of power and value or their skin color, they are internalizing evil and making it their responsibility. But this evil, present in their beings, is also in a certain way independent of any of their actions.

Sometimes guilt appears as a chastisement waiting in the wings, as if God or the spirits of ancestors who seem to be guiding the world (very important forces in some cultures) are unhappy with us. It is as though, without even knowing it, I was wrong in some way; I did not perform well; I have not accomplished what I should have. This is why I am now enduring something beyond my ordinary troubles. I undergo evil, and I also undergo guilt like another evil, even if I am not conscious of being responsible for the evil that engulfs me. It is as if I were stretched between two poles, between a bad woman and a good one. It is as if I have become my own prosecutor or my own judge or as if I were feeling the judgment of the world upon me. But who invented the model of the bad woman or the good? Why do we refer, even subconsciously, to these ideals so removed from real life? Why do these ideals become norms for our own judgment? Who created them? So many questions without satisfactory answers.

This involuntary force in the culture, this place where the exercise of liberty and the search for happiness are chancy and constrained, limits the exercise of my freedom, my choice, my desire for pleasure and happiness. Everything good that I long for is limited by this milieu that keeps me from living with dignity and from escaping the alienation in which I live. This force passes into me like a personal and social guilt. First, in my own eyes I am not in tune with the model I would like to be, and second, in the eyes of the collective in which I live, I feel myself judged. From this, the personal and collective character of my guilt has moved to my innermost self. In this situation guilt shows another face. It is not a moment of subjective recognition of a fault actually committed, not even collective recognition of responsibility for something that turned out badly. The guilt women feel becomes itself an evil, a burden, some overwhelming weight they cannot accurately describe. Such is the case of societally imposed guilt, which is occupied with sustaining a system that produces violence. The patriarchal system in which we live needs to cultivate guilt in us, not guilt based in the reality of our existence or our responsibility, but the guilt of not measuring up to the ideal, whether of the self or of some situation impossible to achieve. It is a stereotypical, pre-fabricated, ideological guilt.

The ideal situation or the ideal image of myself functions like a courtroom handing down a judgment that considers every aspect of my existence. It does not act from religious knowledge or ethical consciousness. It acts like some irresistible force carried along today by means of mass communication, the accepted culture, religions of duty and order, systems of political and economic power. It enters my life with the education I receive, with the culture in which I live, with my personal history. I receive it and reproduce it in my relationships without awareness. It becomes a cultural background in which I live and enter into relations with others.

The culture has reared me in such a way as to understand that certain things are my responsibility as a woman. Everything that has to do with the household, food, care of children and the sick, and making the home a pleasant place—all these are my responsibility. The culture is busy producing in me, through guilt, a control mechanism over my autonomy and my creativity. If I do not live according to this ideal, I am unhappy. The culture forms me according to an ideal of beauty, goodness, and virtue. Obedience to culture is presented as the key to my happiness, but such obedience is only a substitute for happiness, or, in other words, not happiness at all. To obey makes me miserable and to disobey makes me guilty.

How can we get out of this hellish circle of condemnation? How can we reach the threshold of freedom in the midst of this game of life where the odds are already set? How are we to recover the positive aspects of this human construct of culture? This recovery is one of the tasks of feminism as it attempts to understand female guilt and to reconstruct new human relations that do not ignore the conflicts at the heart of every human being and thus of every human relationship. Human frailty may create obstacles to this reconstruction, but frailty or limitation is not a synonym for wreaking injustice. Instead, the effort arises to grasp the mechanism of the patriarchal understanding of the human person, to "deconstruct" the theory that accepts injustice among beings, and to propose concrete ways of improvement, starting with daily life. These ways begin with simple things: awakening the sense of my value as a person; thinking about the traps of consumerism, the pitfalls of the globalization of culture, the idolatry of the perfect body, the necessity of companionship in times of joy or sadness; organizing concrete actions for solidarity and justice on a grand scale, and so forth.

Women's group efforts tend to reduce false guilt while at the same time stressing our responsibility to change human relationships for our happiness and that of those we love. Groups of women reflect on the "objectivity" of their subjective guilt, that is, on what it is that makes us feel guilty; it is a matter of thinking about one's life, taking it into one's own hands, and learning to act with justice, including in the relationship with oneself. Feminist positions are not fixed in advance. No one theory exists ready-made, suitable for application. Instead, there is a wager, a hope, a discernment to make in the face of each situation, always with the risk of failing or making a mistake. Professionals will probably say that women's groups are relying on utopias founded on alienation from their own selves, since postmodern science has decreed the end of utopias. But for us women, who have now found our voice long reduced to silence and our bodies reduced to the pleasure of others, it is good to live for utopias, to hope beyond all hope, and to be with others in the excitement of new relationships of justice.

CHAPTER 3

the evil women do

A victim does not become virtuous by being victimized. She is not an ethical being acting for the common good or for her own personal good by being or having been a victim. Victims, when they cease being victims, or even when they still are, often make others victims. As Zygmunt Bauman says, "As a rule, victims are not ethically superior to their victimizers; what makes them seem morally better, and makes credible their claim to this effect, is the fact that—being weaker—they have had less opportunity to commit cruelty."[1] This harsh statement opens one more window for reflection on evil and women's experience. In a patriarchal society, not only do women endure evil, but they may also be responsible for it in their own way.

It is necessary to denounce the injustices women suffer, but we must not forget they live in the same human reality that embraces us all. The difference observed between the sexes is not a difference in essence. Thus it is necessary to go beyond a metaphysic of the human being, good or evil, and insist on the historical nature of evil we all can see. In actual events we can grasp the richness in diversity and the poverty of evil, its forms of violence, its miseries, and its many faces. And in the human wretchedness of the victims we can read their desire for revenge and their anticipation of making evil pay for evil. This human admixture of good and bad, tied up with the necessity to live and survive, presents itself in different ways in the lives of witnesses (see chapter 1).

Even while acknowledging the suffering of these women, we can detect in some way, directly or indirectly, that they have also themselves committed immoral acts. That evil touched them does not mean that they are exonerated from bad behavior. We may not be able to identify female Hitlers, Pinochets, or other terrible dictators, since women have not had much access to political power. I would not declare, however, the greater goodness of women, even though I do recognize our special value of and respect for life.

In this chapter, taking up the broad points already outlined, I want to show how gender enters into evildoing in certain particular ways. In other words, any evil undergone or committed is stamped not only by class, race, and culture, but also by gender. We need to take account of this variable when we try to understand what often escapes us. Evil is an occurrence marked by one's situation as a man or a woman, by the powers at play in this relationship, by the assignment of work, and by cultural and religious customs springing from these relations.

Women Weaving the Cloth of Evil

If we speak of evil endured by women and use the concept of gender, we must also speak, however briefly, of the evil done by women. They are not only victims but also responsible for evil that destroys or harms human relations. Victims commit evil proportionate to the scale of their responsibility. Structures of violence reproduce violence in concentric circles; violence appears with many faces and in many forms.

What is deceptive from the Christian perspective is that forgiveness, whether preached or imposed by symbols, does not automatically result in healed relationships or acts of violence now under control. We can note sadly that the specter of our dehumanization always reappears under different disguises. The moral path of humanity is marked by obstacles and setbacks. We have no consistent record of humanity's progressing in virtues and moral values. Instead we have the impression that at each moment of our history, we have to learn all over again the meaning of giving and receiving respect.

A feminist perspective does not stress women's goodness as opposed to the evils they encounter, but it does recognize the contradiction and paradox of evil in every human life, even in situations of extreme alienation and injustice. Feminism's efforts toward a more just society are simply a desire, a dream that includes building dynamic relationships always in need of improvement. We are not guaranteed a final victory or a humanity that will ultimately be reconciled with itself and the earth. Clearly, however, hoping for a more just society is an indispensable condition for accomplishing ethical progress toward this ideal.

For women the special place for committing evil is the place where culture has placed them, that is, the household. Here intrigues, plots, lies, and special forms of violence see the light of day. A private scene of evil is combined with the more visible and powerful public arena. While what we say about the private sphere is still in large part true today, this situation is changing not only because of the feminist movement but also because of the remarkably increasing entry of women into the workplace in the public sector and in national and international politics. Consequently there is a growing mixture of responsibilities and duties, especially in countries where the social division of labor is not so limited as it used to be. Still, the home continues to be the place where most women's lives unfold, and this is particularly true in Latin America.

In her novel *Like Water for Chocolate* Laura Esquivel shows how family customs, even if they are oppressive for women, are observed to the letter by women themselves.[2] Mothers have the duty to see to it that they are observed. One of these customs, in vogue at the beginning of the century in Mexico, was that the youngest girl was not free to marry because the duty of caring for her parents in their old age fell to her. That is what happened to Tita. Her whole life she had to tolerate the dear and tragic presence of Pedro, her beloved, who married her sister and lived in the household. "You know perfectly well that being the youngest daughter means you have to take care of me until the day I die," says Mama Elena to Tita.[3] The authoritarian presence of her mother accompanied Tita throughout her life. Even after the mother's death, her ghost acted as a guilty conscience that interfered with the few pleasures life granted Tita. The phantasm of her mother continued to arouse fear and guilt even though, in reality, she no longer had any reason for feeling that way.

Women, feminists must admit, can develop the same cruelty and jealousy that produce systemic violence in society. This cruelty appears particularly in families where the role of the mother in raising the children is more powerful than the father's. Often fathers have a minimal, sometimes even nonexistent, role at home. The mother oversees the reproduction of the family not only biologically but also culturally. Some women imitate in the home the most fundamental social structures. By their presence at home, at school, and in church, they guarantee that the laws of the patriarchal system will continue. They have an extensive educational role, which is also a role full of contradictions. This is the reason that Jean-Jacques Rousseau and later Auguste Comte stressed the role of the woman as the ethical role par excellence.[4] Because women historically have operated outside the economic and political competition of society, they were seen as less contaminated by societal evil. It was necessary to preserve and protect them so that society itself might be protected. This mentality produced not only a separation between the public and private domains, but a separation in women themselves. Women were the protectors of the family and the transmitters of the customs of society, but they were also "public" women in a pejorative sense. Thus a division was imposed between them as if, on one side, one could find the world of purity, and, on the other, the world of impurity.

While social class was one factor in this division, an ideological and cultural concept determined not only women's domestic and public roles but also the ideal female image—the good mother or the role model. The identities of the individual women who reinforce what the patriarchal society needs for maintenance and continuation are not important: the ideal woman helps keep in place a certain social order, a certain social hierarchy, and a certain ethical setting considered the most correct. Prostitutes, single mothers, black and indigenous women, and lesbians were not and are not regarded as models to follow. Both men and women practice this discrimination. You must not be like "them," mothers tell their well-bred daughters. Through the education they receive and pass on, mothers imitate conduct that reinforces their superiority over others. To gain societal acceptance, it is not enough simply to be a mother; one has to be a mother who follows the rules established by those in power.

The patriarchal hierarchy is built on this specious ethical division between human beings just as is the allotment of labor and other human activities. This separation has provided, as we know, a source of societal, psychological, and cultural disequilibrium.[5] It manifests not only the presence of injustice in human relations but a limited knowledge of human conduct and psychology. We know how women who live in a domestic world, so often shut off from the wider world, are capable of stunting the life of their children and even their husbands through an excess of devotion. This overprotective dedication not only makes them think that they know the best and only way to bring up their children but encourages them to devote themselves to the disastrous duty of meddling in others' lives in order to see to their own happiness.

The mother who is not obeyed, even in her foolish whims, presents herself as a victim of her children and blames them for her unhappiness. A vicious circle of victimization and blame enforces the paranoia of excessive maternal love in conformity with a patriarchal model. Historical analysis shows us how often this experience proliferates evil—bad disguised as good or concern for others—and becomes an accomplice to so many forms of violence. We understand why, in many cultures, popular tradition portrays the mother-in-law as a powerful person responsible for bad feelings in a family. The mother-in-law is the symbol of the overbearing woman who is able to reduce the identity of her children symbolically to herself—she alone knows what is best for her son or daughter.

These cultural observations may be tinged with a male bias, but, even so, these jokes and popular tales contain some truth. They uncover a reality about not only mothers-in-law but also mothers, wives, all women who "devour" others to try to make them adopt their vision of the world. In so doing they stifle the autonomy of their children and become themselves propagators of an authoritarian and intolerant society.

Women of the World

"Women of the world" are those who have entered into the world of men for various reasons and through various means. These women serve men and, in a sense, become almost their equals. They achieve equality by entering society, by competition, by freely using their sexuality and their own access to personal pleasure. The studies of the historian Margareth Rago give a good picture of the role played by certain women of the world, madams (female proprietors of houses of prostitution) in Brazil at the beginning of the century.[6] These businesswomen offered poor young women for sale. Their "products" had to give pleasure to rich men, the consumers who establish the rules of the social game. Women obey these rules, but they also set their own rules of conduct. In this way they too make themselves obeyed and respected, and they also perpetuate in their business the logic of the culture and the market.

In this example we must not move too quickly to the moral issue but simply note how women reproduce the same model of society that excludes them and considers them second-class citizens. In this public activity, games of oppression, violence, revenge, and competition are played every day. For the sake of profit men attack women, women attack men, men attack other men, women attack other women. In such a situation no innocence, no spontaneous solidarity exists among women, even though from time to time one may come in contact with a certain tenderness and mercy.

Rago discloses the attitude of certain men who desire and fear the prostitute known as a femme fatale. She appears to threaten men because of her initiative in making advances, seducing men, and making them dependent on her.[7] It is as if she were taking possession of something that does not belong to her; in other words, she takes the initiative to arouse another's body, to oblige him to buy a product, and ultimately to make him a slave to the desires she has aroused. This is a reversal of roles but one allowed by society insofar as women of the world will almost never obtain any recognition of their rights and virtues.

The language used to speak of these women and their place is significant in its fear and contempt. In Latin America, where these poor women live is often called a cesspool, a garbage dump, a sty, a sewer, a site of pleasure and death at the same time. These metaphors created by men are also taken up by the women to describe their profession. Women use them to extort more money or to draw public attention to their situation in life. Here the scale of oppressions and chain of violent acts prove that evil seems to replicate itself, directly or indirectly. And this violence is mixed in with the events of daily life, no matter the class divisions, genders, or cultures.

In her novel *Arráncame la vida* Ángeles Mastretta tells the story of a beautiful young woman married to a general in the Mexican army.[8] Motivated by an insatiable thirst for power, the general has all those killed, women and men alike, who represent a threat to his political or even his personal projects. He seduces young women, uses them, and keeps or rejects them as he chooses. In spite of her suffering and her solidarity with her husband's victims, his wife, Catalina, never publicly denounces his murderous acts. The weight of his crimes and the need to safeguard her own privileges hinder her from taking a stand against him. She settles for living with him without loving him while she loves others, inwardly reacting to his conduct but never taking any radical stand in his presence.

Without making rash judgments, we cannot help noting the complicity of this woman and others like her, not directly participating in injustice and violence but involved all the same. It is as though domestic complicity were essential to maintain public violence. Within the structures of violence and social injustice, women appear as allies, and the home becomes a place of private and silent consent to larger acts of violence and injustice.

Religion, Violence, and Women

Violence against women is also present in religion, especially in Christianity. A striking example can be found in many convents where mother superiors play the role of spiritual guides to Sisters entrusted to their care. In a certain way they become the mouthpiece of male institutions and often govern their convents in their name. The imposition of sacrifices, punishments, and fasts have been some of the means of keeping body and soul under the control of God: God was supposed to control bodies through mediators, that is, through representatives of his will. Hence the role of the mother superior. With some exceptions, these women played the role of guardians of the patriarchal order inside their convents. Indeed, even illicit means of control were considered benign and acceptable in view of the "nobility" of the cause. Superiors often practiced an ethic that divorced means from ends.

In this regard, we must recall the collusion of the superior and the other Sisters of the Convent of St. Jerome with the Inquisition in the proceedings against Sister Juana Inés de la Cruz. They did not refrain from intrigues, suspicions, jealousies, or lies while promoting the illusion of protecting God's justice and truth. Women religious are not known for welcoming differences, highly endowed intellects, or those with special gifts. Furthermore, the theology of religious life, derived as it was from men's reality, has never served as a source of freedom for the majority of women living in convents.

The proposed quest for holiness has been for many a path of sadness, guilt, humiliations, and sometimes violence.

The vows of poverty, celibacy, and obedience, which form the structure of institutional religious life, seem to me to be vows born of male experience. Men in particular have known the corruption of power, ownership, and sensuality. They have observed that these areas distance them from the spirit of the gospel of Jesus; therefore, they established religious life as a restoration of Christian life. In this understanding the vows aim at reestablishing balance and justice in relation to what is impure. In contrast women, who have been under the power of their parents, brothers, or spouses, have not had access to pleasures of the flesh and the taste of power. Choosing the ascetic life has been for women one way of freeing themselves from the hold men have over them.

Religious vows as established over the course of history have been adapted to men's reality. Women have accepted the experience of men as if it were their own and in certain instances have been much more rigid than men. As the conveyors of tradition women not only have obeyed male power but also have made themselves into intransigent power figures in the image of those men who were their models. In their exercise of power, women religious have often been accomplices of the powerful of this world and have reproduced in their convents the same hierarchy and exclusion common in society. We need only recall the presence of social classes within religious congregations, a situation reinforced by the national culture. What is clear, in any case, is that often some women hold on to their privileges while others become their servants. These observations lead us to acknowledge that the same patriarchal structure intersects all institutions of society and reproduces itself in a sick and dangerous way.

We need to remember another kind of violence frequently occurring in women's lives. This violence is often legitimated by a culture and religious formation that gives power to women to issue orders to children, to instruct them, and to make them obey. Here women act violently toward their children, particularly when the mothers are unhappy in their own lives, whether in relation to their partners or for other reasons. Females live first as girls under the violence of their mothers, then as women under their husbands or companions. Several kinds of violence intersect and increase in their strength, growing more powerful especially in the context of poverty, particularly with mothers living in poverty. Doubtless there are always reasons for the rise of violence; we will not analyze them here. What is of interest is to show that the victims of violence are in turn generators of and accomplices in violence, and that religions, notably Christianity, are compromised on this issue. After examining religious factors connected with maintaining a certain blind obedience, psychologists and feminist theologians have keenly denounced them. Through blind obedience to their parents, children have been victims of abuse and all kinds of torture.[9] We need a penetrating critique of the religious practices in our culture if we want to stop the violence they convey.

The Feminine Face of Religious Violence

Some may object that religion has not often been a place of violence. On the contrary, in view of the patriarchal characteristics of the main religions of the world, religion has been not only an arena for violence but the ultimate justification for violence launched against all kinds of people and both men and women, but especially women.

Religion holds within itself many contradictions. If we grant that the message of religions in general and of Christianity in particular is to guarantee the sanctity of human life while preserving the fundamental value of all existence, it seems contradictory that these same values have been able to generate complicity with societal violence. In this, we have to give up defending religion and theologies and accept the relative nature of all human constructs. This attitude will allow us to grasp at least part of the core of women's suffering caused by the Christian tradition. The values and virtues proposed by Christianity have not been lived out in various cultures in the same way by men as they have by women. If, for some, values and virtues have been able to become expressions of love, for others they have also become manifestations of oppression and humiliation. The concept of gender leads us to the heart of the approach to difference. And difference introduces us to a pluralistic approach to the question of evil—evil endured as well as evil committed.

I want to consider first something essential in the life of faith, namely, religious symbols. The anthropological symbols of Christianity are primarily male. We are to imitate the life of Jesus and the apostles, to be perfect as God our heavenly Father is perfect. We are told to obey our parents, clergy, and other religious authorities. The symbols of love and power are unfailingly male and tied to obedience. A culture of obedience has developed differently for women than for men. We must recognize that the hierarchy in society is a sexual one crisscrossed by others. As the German theologian Dorothee Soelle says, the cardinal virtue in any patriarchal religion is obedience.[10]

In such a context God's power seems more important than God's tenderness and love. In the same way, authoritarian religion carries with it a pessimistic view of the human person. We are not capable of loving, of being happy; through obedience we may perhaps succeed in having a taste of happiness and love. Obedience as a virtue is the symbol of an authoritarian world and particularly a male world. Note that male symbols are presented equally to men and women as models for conduct. But while men find in them images that speak to their actual experience, something that corresponds to the language they know, women must disavow their own experience in order to adjust to men's experience and male ideals. Women's psychological investment in the process of patriarchal religions is much greater than men's. We recognize, however, that it is easier for women than for men to have a loving relationship with Jesus. Clearly, in a homophobic culture, men are also victimized. We must show great respect for the different situations in which people live, the different sufferings they undergo. Each man and woman can find in Jesus the symbol that best suits his or her situation in life. While not analyzing the details of this problem, I want to emphasize its complexity.

As we try to understand women, we must not forget that they are accustomed to dreaming of a fraternal world, not a sororal one. They have committed the sins of men; they are saved through means proposed by men. Indeed, this language conveys the poverty of official Christianity in terms of female symbols, a poverty that reflects a society in which the male model is widespread. It also reflects a basically male system of symbols that bears with it, albeit involuntarily, violence against women. Women are called to obey God the Father, to follow Jesus the Son, and to be open to the Spirit that impregnates them. They are invited to take Mary as the model of virtues, as the prototype of the woman obedient to the will of God. Thus obedience to a male image is idealized.

Still, the word *freedom* is added to submission; that is, one must live in obedience freely rendered. What is the real meaning for women of "free submission"? We are given the image of Jesus suffering, freely welcoming the will of the Father without raising his voice in complaint. How does this obedience play out in the daily lives of women? What model of Father should they obey?[11]

No one ever imagined the degree of violence that has come into the lives of women who have always been urged (and sometimes forced) to obey and to idealize male behavior. Women cannot rise to the symbolic level of effectively representing obedience to the Father. That is, it is forbidden to them to think that a woman can fully represent the divine as a man can. This is particularly the case in the Roman Catholic Church. An anthropological contradiction cries out in patriarchal religions and in their symbolism. Herein lies the origin of various violent actions of women against their own life and the life of others. For many among them, religious obedience has been a source of alienation and oppression, not always personally acknowledged. In Latin America most women are not aware of the oppression they undergo. And even if sometimes they are, they often have no alternative to following this model.

Christianity has bequeathed a concept of human existence stamped by the ever-present obligation of attempting to be a better person and conforming to an ideal image of what it means to be human. We have been exhorted to follow and imitate models and to become what they tell us we should be. If there is anything redeemable in this system, it also surely has its limits. The images already present, that is, already in the culture, are enough to form a person, to situate that person in relational life, and to cause the person to reproduce the same images or the same models. We have not received enough help to re-create or reinvent a better image for ourselves. For example, the message of Jesus on the cross leads us to believe that suffering that comes from injustice will lead us to redemption, to victory over our enemies. For women, the path to take us there is to contemplate the sufferings of this man on the cross and to accept our own crosses. The promises of the resurrection call us to bear our sorrows and humiliations and even to renounce our basic human rights.[12] Through experience we can say how much, in practice, this theology accentuates the victimization of women and encourages them in domestic and familial martyrdom. For men, heroism for one's country is a must, while for women it is heroism for the home. In both cases the emphasis is on suffering and submission.

We must add that the main trait highlighted in the imitation of Jesus has often been his ability to endure pain and to welcome his destiny as decreed by his Father. For me and for other women, the question is to know whether there is any way to understand the life of Jesus that does not stress suffering as redemptive or as the path to salvation. In other words, for women and the marginalized of the world, the question is how to overcome the theory that uses suffering to maintain alienation. While we must still treat suffering seriously, we should try also to redeem it, to transform it into a sign of salvation.

I believe some models of God and christological models hinder the self-determination of persons, especially of women. These models have succeeded in keeping individuals in submission but also in making them promote submission as they reproduce the sacrificial plan of obedience. In Christian tradition love is identified with suffering, and this conjunction has penetrated deeply into Christian life and has often resulted in behavior far from liberating and supportive. Revisiting these facts is not only a challenge for the Christian community but a duty of justice toward those who have fallen on the way, crushed by life and unable to rise because of the weight of their burden.

The evil women do, like everything else in their lives, is manifold. It takes different forms and reaches different levels of intensity. To consider these evils prepares us now for thinking about women's experience of salvation.

CHAPTER 4
women's experience of salvation

Speaking about women's experience of evil leads us to consider their experience of deliverance. There is no experience of evil without a search for release, even a temporary one, or simply a desire to escape from a bad situation. This desire is part of being human, an actual effort to leave a threatening situation. A need to escape is engraved in our bodily reality, in the dailiness of our existence, in the strength and weakness of our choices.

This experience of evil and the desire to escape underlie all the accounts in chapter 1. We are a mixture of happiness and anguish, joy and suffering, life and death. We need now to try to understand how redemption is perceived. What salvation (or salvations) do women need? What do women actually experience as salvation? What are the many paths to salvation that distinguish the uniqueness of each life?

Understanding deliverance within a feminist theological reflection begins by noting its signs in daily life, in what befalls us unexpectedly. In actual fact, salvation begins in the experience of what we call the cross or the daily way of the cross. There lies the site of multiple resurrections. And this place of cross and resurrection is where one discovers relatedness as necessary for all life, especially all human life. An anthropological vision that affirms the constitutive mix of human life guides the discussion below. More precisely this means that we are going beyond the concept of the human being as basically good or basically evil. So when I say "mix," I mean that symbolically human beings are heaven and earth, almost at the same time, happiness and unhappiness, good and evil, joy and sadness.

We live, as we know, a temporary succession of happy and sad events in our personal and collective existence. In an instant, grief, suffering, and death can wipe out our joy in life. And in an instant, which does not have the same length for each of us, misery can change to happiness.[1] This experience in daily life helps us in our efforts to overcome the dualisms characterizing our philosophical and theological tradition.

This anthropological perspective makes a case for proclaiming the unity of the human person in different situations. Unity means unity in our body, our history, and our hopes, one that contains diversity and exists only because it is constituted of diversity. Below I will develop three points based on this complex unity about the deliverance that happens in the midst of the darkness of suffering and daily evil. These points are connected to the Christian tradition, but sometimes they refer to experiences outside the tradition and show a common dimension of human life in different cultures. They are: personal and community suffering (the cross); everyday resurrections; and relatedness as a condition for life.

Personal and Community Suffering

In speaking of personal and community suffering I want to return to daily life. I want to be true to the phenomenological method in its descriptive aspect. The phenomenology of evil as women experience it (as discussed in chapters 1 and 2) has put before us what can be called in Christian terms the experience of the cross—the cross as a concrete suffering, one that is physical, psychological, and social.[2] In this chapter I am not suggesting a new theory of the cross, but I want to describe actual experiences of women, especially in the light of Christianity. We need to define what we mean by the cross and to discover, from a feminist point of view, how to go beyond multiple crosses, without any one of them becoming an absolute.

In the same way, I want to try to grasp how people see succes-sive crosses by successive rescues. This, I believe, is the great chal-lenge facing us today if we are to go beyond fixation on one specific form of suffering—crucifixion—undergone historically more often by men than by women. Male suffering—public suffering in the name of a group—seems to be the criterion for all suffering. In a patriarchal society, male suffering in the form of acts of public heroism has a redemptive role for the country, the nation, the peo-ple. Women's suffering, in contrast, has no such role. It forms a world apart. It is less noticed, sometimes passed over in silence, often forgotten. It has no impact capable of arousing public senti-ment. Even in our language, we speak, for instance, of the brother-hood of the world and rarely of sisterhood (although feminist theologians have begun to speak this way). Language hides the way we consider the male normative and universal.

Various statements about "the man Jesus," who died for us on the cross, highlight even further this patriarchal tradition of exalt-ing male public suffering and the role of the male as savior. I do not intend to criticize the actions and personal feelings of Jesus the man; I *do* propose a critique of the patriarchal culture anchored in this mentality. Actually, we cannot know the personal experience of Jesus, except through the many interpretations made of it, each of which reflects a particular theological point of view. Similarly, at this same level of interpretation, a feminist analysis can engage in a dialogue with other perspectives.

As we know, the ideal suffering of the patriarchal world is not only androcentric but also anthropocentric: it minimizes not only women's suffering but also the violence inflicted on animals and plants and the ecosystem in general. If that has been understand-able, given the conditioning of the past, today we are asked to reconsider our positions if we are to think and act effectively with accuracy and justice, with an eye toward the needs of our times. There is surely an ethical urgency to be willing to render justice to women but also an urgent need to rouse us from the apathy and insensibility so typical of our day. Men and women alike who neglect to fight against certain forms of suffering, on the excuse of powerlessness or some cherished tradition, become accomplices in destroying life. Feminist attention to the cross can open one more door to the possible paths of salvation for our times.

An Instrument of Punishment Becomes a Symbol of Sorrow

The cross, that instrument of torture known particularly in the time of the Roman Empire, has become in our culture a symbol that, in the various Christian traditions, brings together different evils or sufferings. To speak of some trouble as "my cross" is to speak of something that weighs down my life, a burden, something heavy to carry, something I have not chosen. Commonly understood, the cross is always something negative in life, something to get rid of or to have help in carrying. But in spite of this common understanding, the cross as an object or symbol of worship, a reminder of the cross of Jesus, means also a call to restored life, a call to redemption and salvation. Thus the symbol of the cross carries many meanings, sometimes contradictory ones.[3] Christians in an earlier time and place have confronted these contradictions, but even today after twenty centuries, this symbolism is presenting a problem, particularly for some feminist theologians.

Let us not forget the contradictions that have been brought about historically by the use of the symbol of the cross. Ever since the marriage of the cross and the sword in the great Christian empires and in the colonial period, the cross has been associated with the ruling powers. This is a well-known fact. I would like to recall particularly the complicity of the Catholic hierarchy with military regimes in various political situations in Latin America and elsewhere. The symbol of the cross has evoked thoughts not always of salvation but rather of domination. And yet within the Christian tradition, we continue to use it with no thought of introducing a change of meaning despite new human relations.

A feminist theological perspective that looks beyond the crucifixion of one man for the salvation of all denounces using the cross to maintain the oppression of women and the poor. Jesus' suffering on the cross has often served as an excuse for justifying the misery imposed on the poor and especially on women. In fact, their submission to male authority has been presented as a duty based on obedience to Jesus, who was obedient to his Father even to death and to death on the cross. Their sacrifice finds its value there and in the case of disobedience legitimizes their guilt. Disobedience is flouting the authority of God and his representatives, and disobedience is subject to punishment.

Another meaning of the cross is quite current among poor women: the cross is identified with their suffering and a kind of curse—being born female. This idea is deeply rooted in the popular culture of Latin America. The fate of being female is often considered a misfortune. One cannot help noticing how many men (and women too) want their first-born to be a boy—partly because of the idea that the man keeps the family name, but also because a man has more chances for happiness than a woman.

I once conducted a workshop attended by some thirty or so women from poor neighborhoods in Recife and João Pessoa; it was striking to hear how many of them agreed that women's cross was heavier than men's and that there were times in their lives when they wished they were men.[4] For them, the cross was not just the suffering of their daily lives in poverty but also their condition as women. Christianity taught them to bear and even welcome their cross rather than to look for ways to be rid of it.

The cross as fate, like the evil of being female, has not engaged theologians. This is beginning to be a topic, though, for growing numbers of women who are looking to put a new value on their persons and to find dignity in various social institutions. It is also a subject for women theologians working closely with base communities in Latin America. The issue is to recognize that the salvation experienced by Jesus, as well as our own salvation, does not occur automatically through the cross imposed by an imperial power but through promoting relationships of justice, respect, and tenderness among human beings. In this way the cross is temporarily laid aside, even as we know that it will reappear in other forms.

The Cross Mixed with the Resurrection

If I consider certain elements of daily life in the neighborhood where I live, or even in the evidence presented in previous chapters, I am face to face with the actual suffering of people but also with their escape or their attempts to escape. In the midst of trouble there is often the presence of neighbors and friends; often a member of the family or even some stranger is ready to help. Suffering is often mixed with solidarity, assistance, understanding. Even the most abandoned seem to feel, thanks probably to the support of others in distress or even in their own dreams, the desire to get out of their affliction. Some sharing common to the torment or the bad news has taken hold of us and represents some touch of salvation.

This touch of salvation, this desire, or this dream is, first of all, necessary for enjoying simple well-being and is almost always present in human life and, we may say, in all life. It is not just an actual rescue that keeps us alive but also support, like the hope of rescue. There is a personal and collective experience of the cross and seeking salvation for oneself and the child in one's arms, a salvation for oneself and for one's companion who is in the same plight. The cross and resurrection coexist in the same body; in the same body they intermingle and form one element. Crosses are often accompanied by other factors that make them a little more bearable. In one way crosses often contain ways of escaping them. Thus we may say that in each cross there is a dream of escape, often a fragile dream but one capable of lighting the way with a gleam of hope. In the daily life of poor neighborhoods people do want to stand in solidarity with those who suffer, but sometimes the trials of specific individuals consign them to loneliness and solitude. Unfortunately, in our affluent society care for the exploited has not matched our progress in technology and science.

The cross is always a scandal—unhappiness, sickness, desertion, objective and subjective suffering—and we fight against it. We fight it through the presence of others, with the help of those who say "no" to the cross. In other words, the "no" to the cross is a "yes" to salvation and justice and happiness, even as we know that it is only a fragile and temporary "yes." The "no" to the cross can also be a cry without salvation, a call for salvation with no answer. And receiving no answer seems to be what happens most often in these great systems that produce violence.

Precisely in this situation the symbol of the life of Jesus is the most telling for women. His cross does not stand alone; the surrounding community shouts "no" to this assassination, "no" to this crucifixion, "no" to the powers that kill. Women stand around his cross as his friends, caring for his lifeless body so that life will not be further violated. This gesture is rich and symbolic because it leads to life. There are followers, men and women, who declare by their solidarity that unjust death does not have the last word. This is why, in various women's groups in Latin America, the symbol of the cross bearing the body of the crucified is occasionally surrounded by people, children, animals, plants. The cross loses its exclusive centrality in order to appear as an ordinary element of life carried by everyone. The objective is surely to make present through the medium of art what is and ought to be the daily tenor of our conduct. Crosses are always present, but different creative forms of redemption are present too. The Spirit awakens in us this renewed possibility of salvation. There are provisional escapes from our tentative lives. Hope is in our bones, walking along with our steps, breathing with our very breath.

In this case, we are not dealing with the exaltation of an instrument of torture transformed into victory over death, but with shared bread, wounds healed, gestures of tenderness, the straightened posture of a stooped woman, hunger satisfied for the moment, the birth of a child, a good harvest. All these can be held up as symbols of life and therefore of salvation. In such an understanding the transformation of the symbol of salvation, or rather, the broadening of its meaning, becomes an act of ethical necessity. Transforming a symbol is a revolutionary act that can be accomplished by simply returning to experiences that expand life and help us carry our burdens, experiences of beauty and freedom that fill us with the joy of life. Concretely, it means listening to the wisdom of our bodies, even with all its contradictions, because our bodies point out the places of resurrection, the sites of pleasure and the paths that lead to happiness. Based on such concrete experiences, feminist theology proposes a different understanding of the cross. Through a path of simplicity we find a more coherent meaning of existence.

We have claimed that appealing to an instrument of torture as a source of liberation seems to repeat the same vicious circle of oppression and opens no door to a broader horizon, whereas alternatives in life can become actual possibilities for action. Likewise, we need to make it clear that when we speak of the crosses of women, it is not to set them in opposition to those of men or children or the aged but to manifest two significant aspects. The first is the importance of making women's crosses visible or, to change the language a bit, to disclose the sufferings of women so as to denounce, in the manner of the prophets, the violence practiced against them. Further, that means denouncing every form of violence and every kind of attack on the dignity of women in no matter what culture or institution.

The second aspect concerns relativizing a unique type of suffering considered to be agony, the greatest of all suffering. The suffering of the crucified, of a man upon the cross, even if it has become the Christian paradigm of suffering, is certainly no greater than that of prostitutes stoned to death, of a mother whose child is wrenched from her, of revolutionaries struggling for liberty, of so many nameless men and women who have fought for the good of their brothers and sisters. Moreover, the suffering of the crucified is not greater than the mass murder of indigenous peoples, of Africans, Jews, Arabs. It is not greater than that of women who see their children die of hunger because of the greed of those who hold economic power.

Indeed, Jesus of Nazareth, proclaimed the Christ by the community of believers, keeps his cross as a distinctive and unique sign. We are not denying this personal and historic aspect. But in the foregoing perspective, this cross is not greater or lesser than others, even though it is a cross of an innocent man. It surely represents a reference to a community of faith, but it must be set in dialogue with others if it is to avoid manipulation. I understand very well how this idea will upset certain male theologians. In their view, symbols and affirmations, like the centrality of the cross, are non-negotiable.[5] But this centrality, absolutized on a theoretical and practical level, becomes a way to exclude other sufferings.

The Canadian theologian Elisabeth Lacelle and other feminist theologians like Rosemary Radford Ruether recall a significant event that caused an uproar on the subject of the crosses of women. In 1984 in the Episcopal cathedral of New York, the Christian artist Edwina Sandys exhibited a crucifixion scene with a woman, Christa, as the Christ figure. It caused a scandal.[6] This work of art, which intended to represent Christ (*anthropos* according to the New Testament) as bearing in the flesh the suffering of women, was considered a pornographic sculpture. Why should the naked body of a crucified man be an object of veneration while that of a woman be judged pornographic? Why should the body of a crucified man become a symbol of reconciliation and that of a woman treated as a cause of separation and argument within the community? Will women by reason of their sex be excluded from any capacity for salvation? What value does the cross have for women? What value has the cross of Mary, who without being physically crucified bore so many other forms of the cross?

It is understandable that a patriarchal theology will have a great deal of difficulty in abandoning the centrality of the paradigm of Jesus' cross. It appears that the only change allowed might be to acknowledge other crosses along with his cross. On his cross he took up the crosses of others: in this way his cross would have a universal value no one could ever question. There is no lack of good arguments, especially in the historical order, to witness that Jesus was really crucified, not Mary or other women. A certain reading of history sees nothing except what it sets out to see. From its own perspective it claims to be scientific and, by that very fact, eliminates other views. A certain dominant, well-established historical knowledge, while claiming to be critical, falls into a less demanding mode. We observe also that a certain reading of history, done with an emphasis on male heroes or martyrs, tends to overlook other agents in history, both men and women. It is once again a partial history with absolute claims. One recounted historic fact is universalized, one particular gesture is absolutized, and one person becomes the center of all activity. This reading of history exhibits a limited, narrow view of the complexity of historical events. Moreover, this male-centered interpretation, which eliminates the potential for the bodies of women to serve as symbols of salvation, runs the risk indirectly of cultivating in individuals as well as in institutions a certain taste for the cross, a kind of pleasure in suffering.

While not denying the truth of the cross of Jesus and of all crosses, feminist theology contributes to the opening of life and thought to a sense of solidarity, in the cross and beyond it. A feminist perspective denounces a certain male-centered universalism of the cross that has been imposed on different cultures as if this event must be the ultimate model. We risk forgetting our own history and its specific cultural context in order to impose another model as the only truth. Instead, through acts of love and justice we must proclaim the scandal of all the crosses represented by the many forms of violence throughout society. This is the challenge we must take to heart. To cling to the cross of Jesus as the major symbol of Christianity ultimately affirms the path of suffering and male martyrdom as the only way to salvation and to highlight injustice toward women and humanity. All the suffering of women over the centuries of history would be deemed useless by such a theology of history.

We must remember that grief and excessive guilt have been means often used to keep unenlightened consciences dominated by the impossibility of changing relations. Assigning guilt is a powerful tool to create an uneasy conscience, but usually it is of little use in changing actual relationships between people. This is especially true in the case of women, whether they are poor or people of goodwill ready to help the poor. One has the impression that the hierarchical system in some way needs guilt in order to keep its power. Acknowledging one's responsibility does not always mean feeling guilty even if one recognizes one's own complicity by the mere fact of living in the same system. There is progress to make when we speak of collective culpability. This guilt cannot be a weight placed on the back of everyone indiscriminately. Guilt must be the feeling of the guilty and not a feeling loaded onto the innocent. If all are guilty, they are not equally so. This kind of guilt, collectively assigned, harbors the danger of hiding the ones truly responsible, those who by their responsibility in certain directive positions can do more for the well-being of others. Going beyond generalities, forcing oneself to speak of specific situations with specific acts and consequences helps in locating responsibilities and the guilty. One cannot say, for example, that women are as responsible as men in the decisions taken by the Nazis to eliminate the Jews or in the bloody massacres of Rwanda in 1994 or in the Catholic church's complicity with dictatorships in Latin America.

If many have had to bear the weight of different crosses, some have certainly been more responsible than others, just as some have been more affected than others. If we accept a certain kind of evil proper to women (see chapter 3), we cannot generalize it to all women. That fact appears to be evident, and yet it is not, it seems to me, if we consider the complexity of actual situations and the social role of the theology of the cross. I am not referring here to any theologian in particular but to the teachings throughout the ages in churches, catechetics, and seminaries, particularly in Latin America. These teachings have permeated Christian culture to the point of becoming not simply one aspect of the Christian religion but part and parcel. Sacrificial behavior is often imposed in every domain of human activity.

Mentioning the cross, then, means mentioning crosses. And when we speak of crosses, or more precisely of sufferings inflicted by some on others, or simply of suffering as the lot of every human life, we always need to speak in the plural. From the moment we speak of crosses in the plural, the cross of Jesus becomes one among many, even though, as classical theologians would say, his is the cross of an innocent man.[7] Is it not precisely the innocent, the marginalized and excluded, and those who fight for justice and human rights who often bear the heaviest crosses, the most paradoxical ones?

One cross cannot contain all sufferings or all crosses. It would risk founding an empire of suffering, even if the end were to found the empire of love. Absolutizing the cross of Jesus is completely understandable in the context of the political theocentrism of the Middle Ages, but it has become problematic in our actual history. Even if we speak of God crucified, we deal with absolutizing one particular type of suffering and one type of manifestation of the divinity.[8] Hence the importance of holding the memory of the crucified Jesus together with the memory of others crucified, men and women alike.

Has it come to this, that we must give up the cross as the supreme symbol of our faith? The temptation is to say "yes" even as we recognize the limits of this statement, not only in the face of a culture of the cross and of sacrifice, but also before the positive fruits of love and devotion that the cross of Jesus has been able to evoke over these two centuries of history. Can we then get out of this impasse? I would rather answer "yes and no" to this question in order to try to maintain the tension between what we want and what is possible. We need to treat these questions with delicacy, without hurrying people's beliefs, without doing still more violence to our culture, knowing all the while that this culture rests on a structure that produces violence. To escape this impasse with finesse we need to help each other to see not only the results of our behavior but also the way to make our most profound beliefs explicit. This is a matter of healing and educating our relationships. It is a redemptive task accomplished by means of a new understanding of the human person, an understanding that opens in us the certainty of how we are relational and interdependent with everything else in existence. This relatedness, which I will develop later, serves as a foundation for thinking of the cross in such a way as to consider the importance and relativity of all crosses.

We must also acknowledge the crosses that we impose on others and that are not even present in the immediate field of our consciousness. By analogy, I think of the crosses that development has imposed on different ecosystems, the cross of the destruction of the ozone layer, the cross of nuclear war, the cross of a national missile defense system. We are being invited to look beyond the cross of Jesus so that we may think also of a broader and more specific salvation for all creation. These challenges to our thought and action begin with reflection on the cross in the light of feminist theology and other perspectives. These challenges present an invitation to reformulate the Christian tradition in order to confront actual questions posed by various human groups.

Everyday Resurrections

Starting with the phenomenology of evil from a woman's viewpoint demands a methodological and theological coherence. In fact, theological reflection must adopt a phenomenological process; that is, it must be founded on personal and collective historical experience, even if it is always open to hope beyond all hope. Methodological coherence means the capacity to understand, through observing the life of witnesses, when and where salvation can be identified. Salvation will not be something outside the fabric of life but will take place within the heart of it. It springs from the expected and the unexpected, from the near and the far, from the known and the unknown. It can last a short or long time. It comes and goes, following the swing of life. Salvation has different origins and occurs at different times, intermingled with the confusion of life. Salvation is what helps us live in the present moment, even when it feeds a dream of greater happiness.

Thus I identify times of salvation with times of resurrection and link them to the crosses of our existence. In Christian language this is to say that a process of salvation is a process of resurrection, of recovering life and hope and justice along life's path even when these experiences are frail and fleeting. Resurrection becomes something that can be lived and grasped within the confines of our existence. As we try to go beyond language that conceives of resurrection as an event following the death of an individual body, we move beyond a certain idealistic theory, springing from philosophy, about the resurrection of bodies and situate ourselves in the concrete reality of our bodies, to love ourselves as historical bodies, bodies that have value today.

Speaking about faith must respect its poetic and metaphorical scope, for no discourse exhausts the experience of faith. Its poetic and metaphorical range prevents us from imposing the limits of an inflexible treatise that might risk betraying its content and openness. But I need to insist that dangerous contradictions are contained in certain talk marked by a dualism, which in the end scorns the historic value of the human being. Talk that refers to a happy outcome at the end of time is able not only to allay the fear of life and death but also to be taken over by the powerful, with a view to dampen any rush toward the liberation of the poor. The powerful always speak of justice in the afterlife; they present happiness as the goal of the journey, as the *beyond* of history. Despite consolations and a certain historic force it has caused, only metaphysical hope reveals these limits. In other words, I am not proposing a metahistorical salvation, but I do draw attention to the different forms of manipulation that this kind of talk has produced.

We need to open a perspective on hope capable of integrating, in some dynamic way, women, men, and nonhuman nature. For this reason such a perspective must arrive at something that is primary, that constitutes our being, that is, our corporal condition, and our consequent finitude. This condition is the beginning of and the basis for a theological reflection founded on the actual experience of a humanity inclusive of women. Even being aware of the foundation of this reflection, we do not have a total grasp of the meaning of the reality of salvation or the resurrection. We simply know something about ourselves, something that we experience, something specific about our deep convictions. We affirm that our being is anchored in this corporeality of the flesh, of earth, of cosmos, and that ultimately this is the first place for every human word about salvation and hope.[9] This means likewise a complete acceptance of our corporal historic reality and of the capacity for finding in ourselves, in this substance that is a mixture of good and evil, the paths to continue to live as members of the body of God.

In practice we must always begin again every day the search for salvation just as every day we have to begin again the actions of eating and drinking. It is a dynamic movement in the innermost part of our lives. This step involves taking another view of the theology of salvation, to see there a redemption in the here and now, a redemption that takes flesh now, even if for the moment this salvation is contained within the limits of our body, our heart, and our daily routine. It is everywhere, even in the hell built by the human person, even in suffering and groans of sorrow. It is everywhere, present under different forms, inviting us to go beyond the evil or despondency that torments us.

But this salvation is not a state one attains once and for all. It is there like a glass of water that quenches thirst for the moment, but thirst comes again, sometimes stronger than before. It is there like a bit of land that one succeeds in acquiring after much anguish, but then the landowner takes over, and there follows drought or the lack of good conditions for cultivating the land. The moment of the hoped-for salvation comes, sometimes seen, sometimes unforeseen. No sooner it comes than it is gone: it escapes, flying away to prepare another and another. This fragile redemption is what we find in the everyday life of every person. Today it is the story of the life and speech of women.

Claiming the dailiness of salvation is not to deny the possibilities opened by a perspective on the beyond of history. We must keep the tension between this historical present, which is our concrete lived experience, and this beyond, which is the object of the tradition of our faith and hope.[10] But we must be careful not to affirm the beyond at the expense of actual history. Women have reclaimed the daily dimension of history and, at the same time, reclaimed the tradition of their own history and the dailiness of the stories and parables of the gospel.[11] There is a whole spirituality focused on the elemental things of life, in friendships, in the little joys of every day that lead to feelings of gratitude and gratuitousness.[12]

Even if we sometimes feel an existential need in Christian culture for a grander and more universal salvation, a salvation in the beyond, it does not come over us when we are crushed by some enormous actual grief, for example, when hunger eats away at our innards or when misunderstanding ruins our relationships or when our child is dead in our arms. Actual experience has a way of changing us, and this is nothing new. It is necessary to add that there is no salvation once and for all, a salvation that would eliminate other problems. We may speak of salvation, but there are only successive salvations in history. Examples drawn from the lives of our witnesses testify to that. No longer is there any unique model of salvation, such as the social redemption proposed by various political parties, or "the way" of salvation proposed by various religions or theologies. Rather, salvation seems to be a movement toward redemption in the midst of the trials of existence, one moment of peace and tenderness in the midst of daily violence, beautiful music that calms our spirit, a novel that keeps us company, a glass of beer or a cup of coffee shared with another. These give us the desire to go on living. Salvation is a bright green garden where vegetables have sprouted after much effort. Salvation is a baby long awaited or a love letter that brings us back to life. Salvation is beauty, a garden on the earth where God walks.

One might say that this idea is of little consequence, that it lacks a political project or social and historical importance, and particularly that it is not theological. But salvation and happiness are lived in our flesh and our flesh of today. Salvation is more than a promise, even if it is already a way out heading toward salvation. Salvation is a get-together, an event, a sentiment, a kiss, a piece of bread, a happy old woman. It is everything that nourishes love, our body, our life. It is more than happiness in the hereafter, even if we hang on to the right to dream of our eternal tomorrow. From this point of view, supposing that we live in a more just social and political system, there is always a dialectic to be maintained between micro- and macro-salvation, between the "already" and the "not yet." Speaking of mini-salvation does not exclude struggling for better conditions of life for all. The private and the public, the individual and the collective live together and are dependent on one another.

If we consider the witnesses in chapter 1, their little experiences of salvation are mixed with all sorts of distress, sufferings, and pain. For them salvation is not a point of arrival but a little oasis in the midst of daily trials. Salvation arrives in the form of a harvest garnered this year in spite of the drought of last year. Salvation comes through the contribution of a doctor, a stranger who succeeded in curing Ruku, or by the job her son got at the tannery. The temporary salvation for Ruku's son came through prostitution deliberately undertaken by his sister. But these individuals and their places, which signified salvation for the moment, have also signified at other times crucifixion, sorrow, death. The same people undergo this alternating experience every day of their lives.

The salvation of Sister Juana Inés appeared temporarily in the friendship of the vice-queen and the vice-king of Spain, who loved and protected her. Her redemption came through her poetry and the theater, through her passion for knowledge and actual manifestations of love. Herein is the contradiction of life and the relativity of all our experiences. Here, too, is the cause of the relative nature of the symbols and metaphors of salvation or damnation.

Along these same lines, we might say that salvation can be an idea or a desire that blocks out present sorrow and gives a person the strength to try to escape it. The idea of returning home gave

Ruku and her husband the strength to continue to break stones in order to earn enough money for the trip. A beggar child, belonging to a group of little thieves, becomes the temporary salvation for Ruku. He is the one to whom she clings in order to continue living, and finally he is the one whom she adopts as her child when she goes home. Temporary redemption, one that gives back eagerness for living, is not bound by moral judgments or narrow laws. It is always open to what lies beyond institutional prescriptions and established customs.

The tenderness of Isabel Allende's second husband and the nearness of her mother become for her the presence of salvation during the sickness of her daughter. Memories of her family in Chile and the spirits of her grandparents help her pass those moments of agony beside her daughter. The decision to write, so as not to die of sadness and despair, becomes a form of salvation for Allende. And finally it is the presence of her friends and their solidarity that sustain her during the hardest times.

Salvation is not outside but mixed in with suffering; it is where one would not think to find it. Salvation is at hand, but we often look for it elsewhere, as if it could be some extraordinary event that might break the inexorable hold of certain sufferings. Salvation is also death, when pain becomes unbearable or when the desire to live is lost for various reasons. Salvation is not a "once and for all" solution but a solution for one time, then another time, and then a thousand times. Salvation is like the breath of the Spirit—it blows where it will and as it can.

The salvation of Carolina Maria de Jesus, her poor little salvation, was the possibility of having something to eat. Her salvation was being able to record in her journal the monotony of her day, happy to be sitting in her doorway and be "watched by the moon." Her salvation was having cleaned up piles of paper and cardboard from the street, selling them, and being able to eat eggs with her children.

The salvation of Rigoberta Menchú is having gained a little gratitude from the indigenous people of Guatemala. But it is a precarious redemption, only temporary, a light in the dark systems of institutionalized violence. Likewise, the salvation of Sister Juana Inés de la Cruz was nothing more than her pleasure in studying, discussing ideas, writing poems, acting, being welcome in intellectual circles in the church of her day. Her salvation was grasped only for a passing moment at the price of great grief.

For the young prostitutes, salvation is finding someone to love them, even if this desire remains only a dream their whole life long. The dream is a form of escape, even when it does not come true. The dream helps the body bear suffering. Salvation for young women is a good table, a home, a family, medical care, respect for their rights, a tender and courteous glance, buying a new dress, receiving a radio as a gift. For most people, salvation is above all a concrete issue, immediate, tied to some actual lack, a suffering that is evident every day, and tied to some evil that seems to be multiplying in history at this very moment. This is resurrection today.

For this reason, it seems to me that salvation is not primarily an abstract and universal idea that encompasses the whole world or only life after death. Salvation is for this daily routine both light and darkness, laughter and tears, in which our life unfolds. It is now that something good must happen in my life, now that my distress must be allayed, now that the pleasure of feeling loved and respected must take flesh in my flesh. The "not yet" is completely bound up with the "now." If pleasure, salvation, or redemption is always delayed, tomorrow becomes an endless frustration. This is not to set up the immediate or the everyday as an absolute, to deny undertakings of great personal and social importance, or to deny the perspective of a world beyond, but to link today more concretely with tomorrow, the here with the hereafter. We are not using faith to bet on the future without trying to taste in the present a certain possibility of what one hopes for in the future.

A thread of salvation crosses all human history, even the history of great sufferings. This thread is entangled with all the threads of existence and becomes the point of contact that allows life to go on. This fragile thread in my existence, in my body, becomes a breathing space, a truce in war, a tender moment when aggression is one's daily lot. This frail thread, I repeat, is often a good meal when daily life is a weak, tasteless soup. It is meeting a friend, a hand held out to us. No doubt it can also be much more than that.

The examples given by the witnesses cited earlier—and so many others—recall the simplicity of the saving acts in the Gospels. These acts are instances of raising to life, restoring sight and life and relationships of justice. These practices are not at all extraordinary since they are written in the ordinary course of life, in the dailiness of our actions, our experience. One shares one's bread, fish, wine; one heals a sick person, draws near to prostitutes. It is a matter of cuddling a child, denouncing those who steal from widows, respecting the dignity of women and strangers. One shares one's table and one's goods; one dances and joyfully drinks the wine of life. All these acts are actual, temporal, corporeal. They are the daily stuff of life, of the here and now.

Ultimately, these ordinary actions, enlarged to collective dimensions, will perhaps become dangerous for those who hold power over others. These ordinary acts call into question societies incapable of taking into consideration the common good over individual selfishness. We can claim that salvation or resurrection strikes fear because it takes place today in the midst of the everyday, in the midst of this present time. The salvation that causes fear is the salvation that denounces our cruelty, our contempt of others, our objectifying human relationships, our capacity for reducing them to merchandise. Sometimes also this salvation, so common and prosaic, is threatened with death through the might of certain people who hold political and economic power.

This salvation, gained along the length of days and in different encounters, seems to be the basis of what we women find in the gospel of Jesus. These simple acts bring us closer to him and to those nameless people in the evangelical stories. By this proximity with ourselves we will discover the proximity of salvation; we will also discover for ourselves a special place of salvation. It is necessary to re-theologize these tiny events of redemption to face up to the systems of salvation that have been established in dogma. Clearly, concentrating on the salvation of one's soul after this life or the resurrection of the body after individual death does not put systems of oppression and exclusion at risk. On the contrary, these ideas run the risk of reinforcing those systems and of giving them the means to continue to produce a false prosperity, which benefits a restricted number of people and countries as well as a false hope for the poor.[13]

We must defy theories of universal salvation, which are easily taken over by great ideological systems and become themselves instruments at the service of these ideologies. The powerful of this world need the omnipotence of God or universal salvation in a unique way to consolidate their power. The universalization of salvation, by the models and language imposed, proves to be a trap today for the daily life of the poor, for indigenous peoples, for minority groups in every culture, and particularly for women's search for autonomy and dignity. I want to speak from outside the yearning for the trans-historic beyond in order to affirm the historic beyond as the first possibility for us who are historic beings. The *historic beyond* is the movement for the hope of happiness for this body, this body that I am, this body rooted in a culture and in time. The beyond is the going past this moment to another and still another. The beyond is not necessarily after my death, even if the beyond includes my personal good-bye to present history.

In its inexorable course, present history has its own consistency in the beings, persons, and events that make it up. This statement has important consequences at the philosophical and theological level. It comes from a new anthropology being forged in the bosom of certain Christian communities, an anthropology that wants to escape the traps of dualist conceptions. Moreover, from the same critical perspective, I am daring to claim that the search for immortality has psychological and existential aspects present in various cultures. There is something that resembles a nonacceptance of our mortal reality, a reality shared with all living beings. Humans throughout the world share a kind of exaltation of individualities and a lack of any sense of belonging to a unique Body, a living Body in transformation—a Body that, as a result, is mortal and open to endless possibilities. But to say "mortal" does not signify an absence of meaning but rather symbolizes the transition of meaning in the intensity of its duration and its mystery.

This mortality in a transformed life would give importance to daily acts of salvation and resurrection. Because we are going away, it is necessary to have tender embraces; because we are going away, people who are hungry today must eat, and I must share my bread. Because this moment is unique in its solidity, its originality, and its monotony, we must live in it with its joy or its sadness. All of this constitutes the theological experience at its peak in the limits of our existence. All of this returns to affirm our limitedness in the heart of a mystery that escapes us and in part to affirm a more feminine human side or one more integrated with the necessity of safeguarding life for all beings.

We still have to ask ourselves: Who will bring us the eschatological salvation? And what meaning does it have? Will it be a great rest in God, a huge happiness, a joy without end, a reunion of lovers whom life has separated? Wouldn't we be creating images in the likeness of our desire for power, stability, and constancy? Wouldn't we be creating illusions for ourselves and claiming that they are essential to our hope? Wouldn't we be creating for ourselves heavenly destinies when, in fact, we are only terrestrial beings? On the one hand, heaven is for us the image of our dreams unified by a beauty we desire; on the other, it is a creation that has become dangerous when it concerns the rights and responsibilities of so many people.

The eschatological salvation of the beyond derives from a presupposition that certain believers or a primitive tradition has affirmed about the continuity of human life beyond death. Eschatological salvation gives meaning when a tragic death or defeat occurs. A death or defeat seems to destroy our present and our hopes for the future. Some people see the tragic death of so many innocents as a human defeat. At the same time they believe in the justice of God (see 1 and 2 Maccabees), which can change death in life. This historical experience was the support for believing in a happy life after this one. But if this experience was once real, today this theological and cosmological model seems to elude us more and more. When we take the trouble to reflect on the events of our current life and on the role of eschatological religions in keeping injustices alive, our desire turns toward the establishing of another explanation.

According to traditional eschatology, all humanity, corrupted by the fall, is in its entirety promised eternal salvation. To the universality of sin is opposed the universality of salvation, and this salvation is imposed by force or, as some Pentecostal churches do, by using radio and television to spread a simplistic and dangerous message. Salvation is offered; it is enough merely to accept it. These churches, like the global market, dominate people and encourage people to become dangerously alienated, often leading to their human damnation in concrete history.[14] In the face of the actual manipulations of the salvation of the after-life, I say that I prefer the known and unknown limits of this earth rather than to fly off to a heaven proposed by theologians but one whose substance I do not know. I prefer to stay enmeshed in the dust of the earth rather than to mount to a sky white and perfect. I prefer, for my last sigh and my last repose, the arms of the earth—which, according to the book of Genesis, is the place where God walks.

Beyond what is imagined by reason, there is something imag-ined by desire, poetry, beauty. This concept of the imagination bets on life without mathematical certitude; it bets simply because life is worth being loved and lived to the full. It is so little, but it is so beautiful! It is beautiful in its fragility, and everything beautiful has something fragile in it and something ephemeral. This eschatology commingled with earth—the cycle of life, the year's seasons, the bodies of animals, plants, and flowers—this human and larger-than-human eschatology warms the heart a great deal. It matters in the being and thought of many women; it mobilizes their art, their politics, their philosophy, their cuisine, their tenderness, their history, and their theology.

I daresay that we women, while having respect for the "kingdom" of God, which epitomizes the ministry of Jesus, do not proclaim any kingdom, because even the notion of the kingdom of God seems to have a face too male and authoritative. We proclaim quite simply the deep desire and the urgent necessity of having our individual and collective body more widely respected. We dream of a tender justice; we yearn for democracy and respect for the res publica. Our theology is one of gratuitousness, one that goes beyond rationalist discourse, bypasses it, does not enter the prison of rigid concepts. We believe in the dimension of "not-knowing," a fundamental dimension of our being, a not-knowing that makes us more humble and at the same time more combative in order to gain respect for differences and the possibility of building an interdependent society. We look for a Wisdom in life, a Wisdom that teaches us to share our goods and the goods of the earth, so as not to have any "needy person" among us (Acts 4:34).

Beginning from this vision, which forms part of our daily life and of our body, we may recover an ethical, fundamental dimension for the life of every being. This is a matter of living an ethic that forms part of the core of the human being, of our body, of our possibilities for tenderness and solidarity, of our questions of every day. This new vision, including both male and female, can be one contribution of feminist theology of Latin America to our Western theological tradition.

Relatedness as a Condition for Life

The third point of this reflection, beginning with the experience of women, leads me to propose a new concept that has not often been used in considering salvation. It is *relatedness* as a reality common to all human beings, to every species, to all things linked to a vital common field. From this perspective, human history is not divorced from the history of the physical nonhuman world.

Human beings do not exist as beings separated from the entirety of beings. There is, Brian Swimme says, a "cosmic genetic relatedness" constitutive of all beings.[15]

I am proposing to adopt this concept to reflect on the problem of evil in order to broaden our field of thought. The concept of relatedness will lead us to thinking of evil as a complex reality springing from different sources, not necessarily bad, and combining with the complex fabric of our lives. It will show us the actual insufficiency of some of our theoretical arrangements deriving from various rationalist systems characteristic of our philosophies and theologies.[16] First we must ask what *relatedness* means in the context of what women experience of evil and then what it means in the experience of salvation, given the perspective taken in this reflection.

Evil and Relatedness

Relatedness is not a subject solely for women and how they view evil. It has to do with everything that exists. The word expresses the living complexity that makes up every single being. It reveals to us a more inclusive and experiential approach to life and invites us to try to understand ourselves in a new way, as human beings forming a part, with everything else, of one same living fabric.

Let me justify my use of the concept of relatedness in studying this question of evil. As I see it, relatedness, dynamic and inclusive as it is, fits the phenomenological method I have taken. It provides a different approach to the problem of evil. Relatedness also provides a different theological approach, to be developed in the last chapter under the title "God for Women."

Relatedness, the way I perceive it, means the connection, the correlation, the interdependence that exists between and among all things. It refers to the very stuff that creates and sustains life, that nourishes life and allows it to grow. When we think of relatedness this way, the image that comes to mind is similar to a spider web, but at the same time more open, more interlinked, everything connected with everything else. This image is defined more by living, interdependent ties than by pyramidal or hierarchical ones, in which everything seems to depend on one sole being. This other way of thinking about the world and the human being incorporates circular images that are not necessarily those of a tight geometric form. They are symbols that invite us to see a quite different organization of the universe and lead us to a different understanding of human beings. In a more circular concept, everything depends on everything else, and if one element is affected, the whole is affected. This is an inclusive image of the biodiversity of all the dimensions of life, a view from within.

Clearly, the idea of relatedness, as I am proposing it here, has much in common with today's ecological and astrophysical theories.[17] This understanding admits of a better way to include varied experiences and viewpoints in resolving a problem. Involving an intermingling, it welcomes surprises more than the model of scientific and theological rationalism allows. In the last analysis, it can be adapted more readily to daily life, to the domestic situation of women in which different realities intersect with one another to make up the stuff of this vital human place. Life is a network of relationships; it cannot be sustained without all kinds of bonds.

Relatedness is more vital than any consciousness and lies within it. A human being is first of all a being-in-relationship, then consciousness, then personal creativity. Merely to observe human life is to take note of how important are all the elements of nature and the global ecosystem in sustaining it. Even before any so-called scientific formulation, one can easily see the wisdom present in all entities that spontaneously seek conditions propitious for their well-being.

Relatedness does not simply have to do with the vital or biological dimension of every being tied to the ecosystem, but also with the ethical dimension. That is why what we call good or evil is also involved in this relatedness. It is precisely this aspect that is of most interest in the problem under consideration. Every culture has tried not only to explain evil but to construct a moral system that tries to make a clear distinction between what is looked upon as good and what is looked upon as evil. And each of these under-lines the supremacy of the good. Some of them identify good with a power or a superior transcendent being called God. In the Judeo-Christian tradition, that being is always good, and if he (it) inter-venes in human affairs, he guards his goodness as something proper to his own being. What is striking, from a feminist reading, is that divine goodness has often maintained a historic masculine face while evil has been attributed to all humans. Still, among humans the symbol of the woman has been much more represen-tative of weakness and of evil effectively carried out.

From this point of view, we might continue to say that evil comes from the human being, from its imperfect structure, or, as Paul Ricoeur would say, from its freedom to do what is evil. In con-trast, God always acts for the good, God is against evil, or, as Adolphe Gesché says, God is objection to evil.[18] It is clear that for every believer, to say "God" is to call upon a presence of goodness, of support, of justice. But God continues to be, in a certain sense, an empty concept, that is, a concept that admits of different mean-ings. I will return to this point later.

I am suggesting that the very imperfection of the human person is what constitutes it, what makes it human. To say "human" is to say "fallible," and *fallible* is not just the possibility of doing evil but also the possibility of doing good. It is here that my thought adds something different to Paul Ricoeur's. He says, "In maintaining that fallibility is a concept, I am presupposing at the outset that pure reflection . . . can reach a certain threshold of intelligibility where the possibility of evil appears inscribed in the innermost structure of human reality."[19] I would say that through the concept of fallibility it is equally understandable that good can be accom-plished by both men and women in the world and only in the world. Fallibility has to do with what we call good and evil. It is as much a possibility for good as for evil, and this shows up clearly in daily life.

Liability to error (fallibility) is what constitutes a human being from the viewpoint of our historical and cultural reality.

Our fallibility is situated in a context of time and place. As much for men as for women, it shows up in different ways, a source of love and of hate at the same time. It is indeed this fragile fallibility that makes us depend on others and that reveals this *relatedness* that constitutes our being. From this perspective, God acts for the good because I define God as acting that way. My talk about God is my human speech about this mysterious reality we call "God."

To say "God" is already to call upon a good "for us." But this mysterious reality always transcends the ethical values that people and religions attribute to it. This reality is in the human and beyond the human. As the Brazilian theologian and psychoanalyst Rubem Alves says:

> The path to God begins by forgetting all the names we have been taught. God does not see directly. He sees only through mirrors. And good mirrors have no memory. They are empty. When we don't stand in front of them any longer, they forget us. If they had a memory, they would retain our face even in our absence. Some other person who would come to look at his or her face would see that face blurred, mixed with mine.[20]

The image of this empty mirror, where images are not fixed in any static manner, is well suited to our discourse about relatedness, about the relativity of good and evil, as well as female images of God. Multiple events and images are faces, successive or concomitant, dynamic, interconnected, even while they maintain a certain autonomy.

At this stage of my reflection I do not propose renouncing the heritage of different cultures and of Christianity, but I am insisting on the relatedness and interdependence between good and evil. This insistence is rooted in a feminist approach to the problem of evil, an approach that contains an inclusive anthropology and ethic as it attempts to remain in touch with the day-to-day experience of women. How can we grasp the reciprocal dependence between good and evil when we have to fight evil and issue a death decree to everything that harms and destroys life? We are entering a universe of thought both simple and complex because it is anchored in a mixture of lived experience.

Evil is the condition for naming the good, and good is the condition for naming evil. Concretely this means that evil does not exist without good, that is, without a good situation that has turned bad or been threatened with destruction. This is true whether it is an issue of an ethical evil or simply of an evil we might consider as natural, like hunger or momentary thirst. Likewise, good does not exist without evil, that is, without some earlier bad situation that had to be overcome for good to appear. In a way, we can say that every situation we call bad has something good about it or produced something good from one moment to another, even if it is only a temporary denunciation of evil. Likewise, situations or behaviors we call good contain evil or something bad. We know that what some people call good is oppressive to others. There exists a control, an imperialism in the name of good, capable of killing lives. This is the reason why we have to say once again that good and evil live off one another and that there is no way to root out the bad growth from the good.

I am not implying an ethical relativism that would allow killing for profit or stealing people's rights through a privileged exercise of authority. But I am creating an understanding of the dynamic of life and its oppositions, with what actually constitutes us and keeps us alive. Without evil we would not know what is good; without sickness we would not know what health is. Without evil we would not be the human beings we are. Without evil we would not know how to give thanks for the good. This is no apology for or glorification of evil but an empirical observation of the complex relatedness of everything in human life.

From the examples that have been given in the course of this phenomenological reflection, what is called evil or harmful was also able to evoke positive reactions, reactions of struggling for life and for the dignity of women. In actuality, evil makes an appeal to good, and the good protects itself against surprises and attacks from bad situations, both expected and unexpected. The abyss is ever-present, and vertigo always accompanies us. This is evident in all religious structures in which the faithful are urged to protect themselves from evil. If evil is not actually present now, that means it has the potential to appear at any time, and one may be almost certain of its presence. If suffering is not here today, living in my flesh, it is nearby and constitutes an ever-present threat.

Observing this mixture of which we are made and in which we live leads us to a different assessment of good and evil. This approach can no longer isolate good or evil as separated from each other, each with its own identity. It restores them to their common history. There was not from the beginning a history of good followed by a history of evil. Our human reality exists as it does because, from the beginning, from our mysterious origin, our innermost self has been created this way. Our cosmic genetic makeup seems to have been so formed from the start. We are what we are, unwilled and willed, good and bad at the same time.

This combination is a condition of human and nonhuman life; in other words, life is both life and death at the same time. Life is fed from life. In order to live, we kill, we devour, we eat, we drink, we digest living things. It is within this situation that we take another look at the question of evil. What is evil? How shall we understand it? There is no doubt that we know it through our bodily experience, through intuition, learning, tradition, culture, but we must always describe it anew.

From a phenomenological perspective, the first thing to say is that "bad" does not exist, but rather "bad things." Putting evil in the plural gives it empirical and historical substance and recognizes the many contextual ways it expresses itself—cultural, corporal, sexual. When we speak of evils, we place the evil in a particular situation, in a time, a culture, a religion, a sex, a difference. This means abandoning a generic discourse about evil and entering into the daily run of what is harmful to actual persons. And what harms the lives of some is not equally harmful to the lives of others. Children experience evil in their fear of the dark or the fear of losing their mother or when they are hungry. Old people experience evil in their fear of death or in loneliness. The poor and the marginalized experience exclusion and abandonment. Prostitutes and the homeless experience contempt. Evil has a thousand faces. And for every experience of evil there needs to be a particular deliverance. Relatedness includes the affirmation of interdependence and difference.

From this point of view we could define evil as an *imbalance* that affects life and makes up a part of it. And this bad disequilibrium is experienced different ways by different groups and individuals. It has its own consistency; it is a presence within us. It is not nothing but something in my life and in the history of nations, even if this "something" is an absence of something. This imbalance affects us in several ways as a personal and collective sickness in our body and psyche. It is a debility that keeps us from living, something from which we seek relief or a new balance. We try to shuck off this disorder in our being, but even as it leaves, it has already announced its return under multiple forms. Concretely, evil is a kind of holding on to life for its own sake, an undue appropriation of goods by individuals and groups who take possession of the earth and of so many other things.

Evil is also a dysfunction between me and myself that leads me to cultivate narcissism and my own interests and to forget that I am in and with others, that I need them if I am to keep on living. Evil is this unexpected sickness that attacks me, takes hold of my body, leaves me to the mercy of others, cancels my appointments, my possibilities for work, and my plans for the future. Evil is having too many goods, concentrating on riches and power, enjoying things at others' expense. Evil is idolatry of the individual, of being white, male, racially pure, of belonging to the chosen people, of women in beauty contests. Evil is asserting the superiority of one sex over the other, superiority that permeates social, political, cultural, and religious structures. Evil is exploiting the earth as an object of profit, as capital, to the detriment of the life of entire peoples. Evil is imposing religions or gods as the only ones able to save humanity. Evil is making people believe that one knows the will of God, that one can teach it or even impose it. Evil is accepting a destiny of oppression without fighting for dignity. Evil is being silent and making others be silent when justices need to be denounced. Evil is losing one's beloved, suffering disappointment in love, being forgotten, abandoned. Evil is both singular and plural; present, past, and future. It consists of experiencing instability in our lifeforces. And it is from within these miseries that good things—experiences of salvation—see the light of day. It is in these vales of tears that joys surge up, that commitments of solidarity take hold, that the powerful end up "brought down . . . from their thrones" (Luke 1:52).

It is amazing to realize that evil has the same source as good, but an excessive good for some because this good is voracious of goods and excludes others from sharing in life. To think of evil this way places us outside what is called metaphysical evil and puts us in the here and now, in actual evil with many faces. This many-sided evil is the evil lived out in human experience and, in this consideration, lived out in women's experience of evil. No metaphysic addresses the subject of evil as women perceive it. This evil has immediate causes, or even distant causes that have brought about its arrival in the present. But this evil has no beginning; that is, no origin, not even a mythic one, can explain it. That is why we have to insist on the fact that it has no specific origin: it is always there, it has always been there, mysteriously woven into the structure of life, killing life and yet allowing it to live.

Evil has no origin, but evils are not without historical causes. Evil is always present, but at the same time it depends on us to stimulate its growth, to let ourselves be contaminated by its virus, to allow it to flourish. Therefore it falls upon us to struggle against the control and influence and power it exerts. I propose that we stop looking for meaning any longer or for a primary cause for certain evils. We will simply have to accept that it is our responsibility to console people and to root out the present evil, such as an injustice or a physical suffering, without trying too hard to make sense of it. Often, certain evils escape our understanding, just as do certain experiences of happiness and generosity.

We need to look again at the anthropological question of evil from the viewpoint of the interconnected nature of all life and take upon ourselves a new responsibility for life in all its forms. In my view, we need to reconsider the key saying attributed to Jesus of Nazareth: "to love one's neighbor as oneself." This commandment contains an ethical relational dimension we need to take note of in everyday life. Redeeming acts will flow from it in the form of justice and wisdom. Concretely, this has to do with balance and imbalance. If we lean too far in the direction of self-love, we easily slip into all kinds of narcissistic behavior, which has as a result the destruction of others or, at the very least, deafness to their cries.

In one sense, patriarchy is a societal form of male narcissism (a love of anything that is like me), manifest in every cultural, political, and religious institution. Thus it is easier for men to fight for any other cause of social justice than for the cause of equal rights for women. In Latin America, recent experiences of the struggle within unions demonstrate how questions raised by women have not received men's support. I am thinking particularly of women's efforts to get day care centers in the workplace or their demands for safe drinking water in their homes. Similarly, in the church-run academic institutions, women have not received men's support in gaining the same right to teach theology. In fact, it is considered an exception if they are admitted under the same position as a man.

Narcissism is boldly apparent in politics and has produced various forms of imperialism, fascism, Nazism, racism, and all sorts of exclusion of the other for the sake of protecting men. Social, political, and religious narcissism is contrary to the values of the gospel of Jesus. From this excessive narcissism we can move to an excess of self-giving, an excessive obedience, excessive humility, silence on matters of social outrage, self-effacement—behaviors that have often been demanded of and perfected by women. This excess, deemed to be a virtue in the patriarchal world, is vicious from a feminist perspective. This other extreme shows us that forms of disequilibrium can exist through a lack, by default. Women have lacked an effective love for themselves; they have lacked autonomy, self-esteem, development of their own mental capacities, the courage to say "no" to various forms of enslavement—domestic, social, political, and religious.

This leads us once again to the question of difference in how values are lived out. What is moral for one person, for a man, for example, is not necessarily so for a woman by reason of different social conditions and situations. This is what leads us to keep ethical questions open to different circumstances and especially to dialogue in order to build up relationships that promote the life of the greatest number of people.

To love the other as oneself has to be understood in concrete situations in which each individual, whether among community, friends, family, or work associates, is ethically obliged to place himself or herself within the skin of the other. A mutuality takes hold and transcends any principle or judgment deriving from already established dogmatic laws. We have to construct among different groups provisional agreements, always capable of revision, in order to allow the common good to be effective, not just a beautiful expression stated in a document, like the Universal Declaration of Human Rights, that lacks any force.

Relatedness and Salvation

The question now is to discover how relatedness can open the subject of evil to a different understanding of salvation when women are included on an equal basis. First to be stressed is that, through relatedness, we open ourselves to a different model of human community, that is, a model over and above the hierarchies present in classical models. These latter are arrangements that always consider the other to be either inferior or superior and therefore inevitably exclude others at every level of human relationships.

If we look at relatedness, we can move beyond the model of humanity perceived as a male body, for example, the body of the male Christ, in which the function of every man and woman is in a line of subjection that maintains a hierarchy. It would be possible to transcend the male symbolism of the body of Christ by introducing an image of Christ as salvation coming from men and women and nonhuman nature. This Christ would exist in Jesus of Nazareth but also beyond him. In similar fashion we can place ourselves beyond the models developed in modern times in which God, at the very apex of the hierarchy of the world, appears to direct the world according to his will. In these models women are on the lower rung of humanity.

A model defined by relatedness sets forth a different anthropology. No longer will it be possible to identify women's bodies with nature and men's with reason or spirit. This kind of dualism will have to be banished because it justifies the oppression of women. No longer will it be acceptable to control the bodies of women, indigenous peoples, and people of color, as if this control over those considered inferior were actually legitimate. No longer will it be possible to develop a historical theory of the superiority of some over others as being God's will. Relatedness opens the way for an interdependent justice, an ecojustice, that is, justice that includes the ecosystem. Relatedness sets forth a search for balance in daily life as well as in the institutions we establish. It shows us that women's sins are connected with men's excesses and that men's sins are connected with what women lack. Such relationships are manufactured and established by culture, a game of strength and power. And because they are fabricated, they can be dismantled and rebuilt.

In this new approach women will not be representatives or symbols of evil. They, along with men, will take responsibility for making this earth a home for all. Both men and women will have to try to understand each other outside the dualistic and exclusive structures so present in our culture.

In their interdependent existence, good and evil would become matters of equal responsibility in history. This is not a question of imagining some utopian world where there is no evil or exclusion or hierarchy, but envisioning and living in a world more balanced, more ethical, more respectful of diversity and difference. It means dreaming of a world where beauty and respect for difference will be able to stabilize human life. Human existence involves a community of beings who dream of love and justice even while sowing seeds of hatred and violence. And it is this very mixture that allows us to live and speak about a salvation tailored to different groups and situations. This is, in broad outline, the challenge that a life-giving approach anchored in relatedness sets before us as we consider anew the problem of evil and salvation.

CHAPTER 5

god for women

My God, my God, why have you abandoned me?
—Mark 15:34

According to the early Christian community, this verse from a psalm was the last cry of the man Jesus on the cross, but this could also be the daily cry of so many people, particularly women, in various parts of the world. The experience of abandonment may best characterize the life of most women considered in this study—abandonment by reason of the evil they have undergone, the sufferings they have endured, the scramble for ways to survive. At the same time, it is an abandonment accompanied by something very fragile that still keeps life going and therefore is of interest at the level of women's experience and also at the theological level.

Here we may ask: How can we develop a phenomenology of the experience of God from a feminine perspective? Using the phenomenological method of letting situations speak for themselves, we look to situations wherein women's cries to God are the loudest and most frequent. Then we shall try to sketch an outline, knowing full well that any interpretation will be only a pale understanding of what women have endured.

This work is not a treatise on God but a discussion of what women experience when they say "God." Further, it is not a general treatment of this experience but a study of examples from literature and actual testimonies. What can we make of these experiences when women cry out to God? What this interpretive study tries to convey is life in its many forms and its complexity. We have to understand, beginning with women's words and pleas, the way in which they view their relationship to this being, this mystery called God. For most of them, it is a relationship not often thought about, a relationship within the dailiness of women's work and concern. It is also a matter of grasping the consequences of this relationship to God in concrete day-to-day living. By beginning with specific instances we will be able to sketch a theological outline. We start with feminist theology, which aims to show, among other things, the relation between women's lived experience in and with God and official theological teachings proposed by church authority.

God and the Daily Experience of Poverty

Sometimes it is a cry of despair, sometimes a lamentation, sometimes an insistent demand, sometimes a long silence or an outburst of joy. Each of these is accompanied by the word *God*, as if something very special lived in this word that could change inexorable suffering, prolong a moment of happiness, or assuage some relentless pain. This experience is certainly nothing new, but it seems to recur in the same way in every century and culture.

To say "God" in the midst of the daily course of women's grief is, first of all, to put these women in a social context but also in a situation defined by gender. This means that their cry to God is like the cry of all the poor and disenfranchised of the world, but with a specific feminine dimension. Women's cry is grounded in their female physicality with all the social relations that entails. Their cry has its own tonality, its own density, its own color. Their cry is the result of the power games in society that affect them directly.

On September 26, 1997, in the French newspaper *Le Monde*, a photo representing the grief of two Algerian women and the agony of a people was published as witness to the irrationality of the evil we cause. The caption read: "This woman who is screaming has just lost her eight children; the one who is supporting her [has lost] her parents."[1] It is impossible to say whether the word *God* was spoken in these cries of hopelessness, but given the religious

Islamic setting of the country, it is quite probable. In Latin America this word, *God,* is part and parcel of the daily life of poor women. It is associated with the care of children, the search for food, looking for work, being sick, and getting well—in joy, in despair, and in hope. The word *God* is everywhere as though it is a part of the breathing and culture of the poor. God appears as a last resort, or perhaps a resource in the midst of everything that makes up life.

"Thanks be to God" is a common expression, as if it were capable of protecting against the worst, as if the worst would surely happen if this invisible protection were not present. In short, God is the ally who will always be at the event, even if what is so ardently longed for (like salvation) does not happen. A surprising persistence vis-à-vis God exists among humanity. Indeed, a great many people, especially women, experience a common frustration from not attaining what they hope for and need for a life of dignity—daily bread. Women often eat the bread of sorrow, even when they may celebrate moments of joy and gratitude. Something like a resistance movement flowers in the midst of sorrow, a resistance by women who actually suffer in their bodies, and by others, too—men and women who are in solidarity and who are themselves vulnerable to the afflictions of this world. To bear pain together is to resist suffering, to find common ways to try to overcome evil.

If the God of women is in their image, that is, poor and defenseless, he is also radically different from them because he is someone who has power, which is marked by a special form of love.[2] To say that God is in women's image means that their experience of God is the image of their world, their culture, their questions. But how does it happen that women, themselves poor and without power on the social and political level, look for a God who has power? How is it that they want the intervention of an all-powerful being and that they call him God, when their daily experience is so different? Do they call upon an all-powerful God, the antithesis of their weakness, hoping that he will use his power to come to their aid?

If, as the prophetic tradition says, to know God is to experience him, what knowledge or, more precisely, what actual experience do women have of the power of God? In the lives of the poor women whom I have met in my study and in the lives of women who live in the countless slums of Latin America (and, yes, of the world over!), I have observed an experience of a power that is totally different. This power seems over and above all known powers; it is simply the power to live! In spite of all the contradictions and paradoxes and even the disaffections involving this inconceivable power, it possesses in popular culture some element of a real savior.[3]

Popular culture, as I am using the term here, is not the culture created by the poor, but the culture imposed on the poor by various institutions and means of communication. In the midst of this world in which there is so little choice and so many contradictions, however, one can pick up this reference to God, perceived as someone who has power unlike any other. The difference seems to lie in the idea that, in spite of everything, someone or something wants the world to be other than it is. And this otherness is a counter-current to present injustice.

But we are not beginning with a mere theory about God. Exterior observation reflects and senses experience, resulting in the creation of a theory out of that experience. A "hope against all hope," like an expectation beyond any possibility, exists as if to say that the last word about life is not about the army and chariots of Pharaoh. Even if armies and chariots (the powerful ones of this world) are historically the conquerors, something else—a hidden well, the shade of a tree, a baby's smile, help given by a grandmother—can give strength and support to those who wish to continue to live. An almost transparent thread holds life together in its many forms. We have here a theology, not a theology limited to the church, but a theology in human life and of human life.

I am thinking particularly of the character Ruku; so few things nourished her hope: a tiny harvest, finding the way home, the help of a beggar. Without saying "God," but turning to the goddess, she offers sacrifices with the hope of being heard. She lives as though her life were supported by a thread, and it is just this thread that allows her to move on.

In the Christian world it is the same. For Carolina Maria de Jesus in her daily struggle to gather paper, only the day at hand matters. Every day she places a wager on life, a frightening proposition for those who do not live in such a situation. The God of poor women shows his face in the transitory and in the life at home. He is a God called upon to make life go on, especially in domestic matters. He is a God called upon in the red-light districts, when prostitutes are afraid of their clients or of the police. Women call upon God to find food, to cure a baby, to bring up a child, to send a husband home, to get out of trouble, to have some little plot to plant, to get a house. It is not for war, for some political victory; it is not for great global economic enterprises. God lives in the house, or even in the street if that is where the domestic battles take place. He is present in tears when there is no bread, and he is present in the joy of having something to eat. It is in this way that God is in their image, that is, that he enters into their daily life problems, makes himself present in their world even while he possesses power beyond their world. This is the theology not considered important, that is, the possibility of affirming a hope, a dream, a wish, a sigh, a desire that opens up the world and introduces alternatives, even little weak ones.

In this daily life of women, scarcely ever is there heard any case against God. The truth is that there is no reckoning of accounts with God when prayers are not answered. People are always asking for things, but he can refuse to grant what they ask for. There is a submission to life on God's terms in spite of contradictions and paradoxes. This is part of the logic of the culture of the poor. God does not give answers to theoretical questions. God simply sustains life, is in life, is in us at every moment. Besides, one does not have the time to pose complicated questions to him!

From the domestic world of poor women, I am moving on to another reality, one also on the domestic horizon but organized quite differently, a reality with a different logic and other concerns. It is the domestic scene, public in a way, of the convents of women in New Spain, a scene that offers work and an honest livelihood to so many women without status in this corner of the world. There one enters through a narrow door, ready to understand a different language, born of a particular historical and cultural context. One feels uprooted from one's country, even though, here and there, songs, poems, and thoughts awaken familiar memories. One must enter without being certain about understanding the intricacy of this world. One must enter with a certain inner fear, a form of respect owed to notables with a history of enigmas, sorrows, and tenderness.

God's Baroque Face

To speak of the experience that others have had of God is, we know, a difficult task. It is difficult enough for anyone to speak satisfactorily of one's own experience. What, then, can we say of others' experience of this ineffable mystery? What can we say about what has been written in a time and context far removed from our own? I approach this topic timidly, like something sacred, something of which I have faint intimations, something whose depth I suspect and whose originality I fear to trample on. Even more, to speak of Sister Juana Inés de la Cruz's experience of God is a delicate and dangerous undertaking. We must put her in the baroque ambiance of New Spain, one not familiar to me, but one I must at least try to enter in order to understand something of what she underwent.

Her work reveals, all of a piece, her personal experience, the art of poetry she learned, the theology of the church fathers and of Thomas Aquinas, as well as the theology of her own day, which she knew well. Speaking of others' experience of God is difficult; a particularly complex case is that of Sister Juana Inés de la Cruz, who consciously trained herself to be a poet and literary figure and, to this end, became a religious. Her main objective was not to speak of her experience of God but to be an artist, to accumulate knowledge, to teach, to please, to converse. Although she says in *The Response,* "I don't recall writing for my own pleasure except for a little piece titled 'The Dream,'" Octavio Paz remarks emphatically, "We shouldn't let this deceive us: it is her longest and most ambitious poem."[4] She wrote the poem in self-defense in answer to charges brought against her by the bishop of Puebla, who accused her of busying herself with profane literature and poetry, considered a violation of her state as religious. To justify her art, she displayed her knowledge, citing authors, handling Scripture with ease, and recalling the Magnificat, a poem, she pointed out, written by the Blessed Virgin herself.[5] The Virgin as poet is excuse enough for the artistic route Juana Inés travels. In response to criticism that caused her grief, she used her knowledge as a way to try to convince her opponents. We do not know her intimate feelings; we can only imagine them. She did say, though, that her gift came from God. In the midst of her suffering and persecution, she wanted to demonstrate to others the strength and marvel of this gift. Through her poetry she seemed to experience God in her own way. God seems to have been her direct inspiration and the one who symbolically became the poem itself.

De la Cruz claimed she did not write for her own pleasure but for others'. She put at others' disposal her art and vast learning, so uncommon in the women of her time. Can we really believe that she did not write for her own satisfaction? Pleasure for women, especially for women religious, was forbidden. For this reason humility made her hide her pleasure, her pride in being a poet, the joy of possessing in herself this divine gift. We know that baroque poets want to evoke astonishment and wonder, want to discover secret resemblances between things, to unite them, to work them into a poetic form. Her concern is not to express what she feels, to lay bare her subjectivity, but rather to deal in forms, to hide herself behind her poems, and to reveal as little as possible her own feelings. Similarly, the baroque poet sings of others, speaks of others as if a great distance exists between the author and his or her characters. As Octavio Paz says, "The baroque is intellectual and active."[6] It is full of colors, of verbal abundance, of metaphors, of different forms. The subject almost disappears and concentrates on objects or others.

The poetry of de la Cruz transcends national boundaries. Not only does it reflect indigenous culture and creole sensibility, but it integrates sacred Scripture, theology, Greek literature, and European contemporary writing. She composed her poetry for others—pupils, clerics, and friends, especially her friend the vice-queen Maria Luisa Manrique de Lara of the court of the vice-king of Spain.[7] It is difficult to grasp the sorrow or the joy that infuses her poetry, even though the reader guesses at the emotions or positions she wants to defend.

To have a better grasp of the person behind her poetry, we need to interpret her writings using modern methods of literary analysis, which will allow us to discern the contextualized subjectivity of her poems. But these methods also risk misinterpreting her intention, her context, and her baroque art, which are marked by the constraint of hiding intimate feelings. Thus, speaking about her experience of God, particularly her experience of evil, uncovers from her life only what she intended to reveal; we must guess at the rest. Her most profound experience of evil, that is, the silence imposed on her in regard to her intellectual work, we know through intermediaries. We have no direct knowledge of her thoughts after she was reduced to silence by the Inquisition two years before her death. We do know that this suffering led to her death. Her God, the one who gave her the gift of letters and science, is not victorious. He dies in the suffering of Sister Juana Inés de la Cruz.

In analyzing her writing, we find that important insights into the meaning of life do not come from her religious poetry but from fictitious characters, like Fabio, whom she created and in whom she unveils her heart. For example, in *Liras* 211, she writes:

> Beloved, my master
> hears something of my tired moans,

woven by the wind,
which will bring them to your ears,
if the sad accent does not vanish
like my hope in the wind.
Hear me with your eyes,
Because your ears are so far away. . . .[8]

What are her plaints, her actual sufferings of the moment? Why does she insist, in this appeal to God, on her Love so distant, so deaf and blind to her distress? We know that her sorrows are there, mixed in with her artistry, even if we cannot name them in any direct way and even if we do not know them in an explicit form.

The verse that follows introduces a section on the birth of Jesus, but its meaning seems to transcend the praise appropriate to this birth. It brings us into the hidden and paradoxical dimension of faith, but with an introduction subtle and delicate.

How does it happen, my God,
that I believe in You,
and even more, believing what I see,
I do not see everything I believe?[9]

The game between seeing and believing, so brilliant and full of doubt and finesse, becomes a refrain in her poem. But it says nothing directly of her own doubts. She never affirms her doubts in a clear, rational discourse. We discover them mixed into her poems and literary writings. She does not speak explicitly: her formation and context do not allow it.

In the verses that follow, de la Cruz leads us into the spirituality of the marriage between a woman religious and Jesus Christ. This is a composition for a feast day. We might say that it is an old theme, worked in the poetic baroque style, as a dialogue between two hearts. The theatricality of the situation hides its deeper meaning but reveals a bit of the spirituality of her day as well as the impressions left in her formation by various literary and spiritual currents.

Come to the Feast, come gentlemen,
given that a young woman is getting married, and it is for love!

> She is beautiful and filled with Beauty for him;
> And he, he is a red carnation,
> She, in her love, makes her first entrance
> And He fills her with gifts.
> Come to the Feast, gentlemen come![10]

Without suppressing the erotic dimension in this wedding song, she continues in the same vein:

> Come, mortals, see my pleasures,
> and celebrate with me my joys:
> today my Spouse sets me among his shining thrones,
> His Blood makes up my cheeks,
> milk and honey his mouth gives me.
> Play, play,
> Celebrate with me all my joys,
> that today I know myself to be Spouse of Christ![11]

While these poetic verses partially reveal her personal experience—the experience of someone who enters into "sacred letters" and wants to become recognized and appreciated—they hide her daily routine, her boredom, her malaise, the persecutions she endured, and her innermost reactions.

Her silent cries to God were heard only after her death. Her critics and commentators have enabled her writing to be heard and appreciated. Recent feminist authors have put aspects of her life and work in a new light.[12] Thus her suffering and her silent lamentations did not gain recognition until several centuries later. She weeps in us today; she makes known her existential doubts in us; she criticizes the society of her times in us. We take her as our sister in our own trials, as a pioneer of the past and as a symbol of autonomy for women of the present. Sister Juana Inés de la Cruz calls us to an experience of freedom in word and act. She urges us not to accept silence when it is imposed and to dare to feel and think of God as part of our own bodies, our experience as women, our history, and our culture.

God in the Absence of God

After Juana Inés de la Cruz, whose sighs are veiled by poetry and rhyme, another woman's voice clamors to be heard—that of Isabel Allende. This time she is our contemporary, crying silently to God in the midst of her struggle for the life of her daughter and for her own life. How does one speak of God when it is not one's practice? How does one seize the mystery of his presence in the ambiguity and contradictions of existence? How does one express this presentiment of mystery without naming it in some precise way?

Allende tells of this mystery in a special way, with a different language, one that searches for meaning without a theological vocabulary. She gives herself over to the mystery of life, letting herself take hold of and welcome the fact that we must accept certain things in life. During her daughter's illness and shortly before her death, Allende had a dream in which her daughter asked to be allowed to die. The words of her dream seemed to give strength to her weakness and her sorrow and also to embody an acceptance of mortality.

God in the absence of God—this is the expression I propose for speaking of Allende's openly agnostic position. She does not know how to say "God," but she welcomes those who do say "God" or who appeal to the spirits or various aspects of nature to help her save her daughter and to let her daughter depart. In face of the fragility of life and the ever-present threat of death, she finds every means acceptable to maintain and heal life. Her experience opens us to an understanding of God as something unforeseen that can change the course of things but in her case has not changed it. Reality resisted her struggle, and in the end she had to agree to accept it, to say *yes* to this mysterious path of the living.

The unforeseen belongs to no one. And for this reason Allende allowed religious, "wonder-workers," the prayers of her mother to be present in her life, while her daughter was dying in the hospital. On a personal level, she felt far removed from them, but at the time of a loved one's death, it is not good to count too much on personal doubts. She seemed to feel that not a single resource for restoring the life of her daughter should be lost to her, even those resources that belonged to a line of thinking different from hers.

Allende's experience returns us to the divinities of the earth, as if what we can touch, smell, and breathe becomes the most concrete divine reality. This is something like a primitive experience, more fundamental than any description of it, the experience of being of the earth and of returning to the earth. The earth appears as our familiar, something we know, our own substance, mother, or primary source, capable of giving us peace and helping us to consent to the mystery of life. The leading thread in Allende's actions, in a religious sense, consisted simply in opening herself to all possibilities that could assist life. A kind of religious eclecticism came over her, demanded by the drama of the illness and the proximity of death. She was not concerned about her own convictions but rather with finding whatever way she could to save Paula's life. If the beliefs of others could bring some consolation for Paula, she would accept them in order to bring her daughter relief. No choice was more urgent than trying to save her daughter's life. Even without saying it in so many words, for Allende human life was worth more than all religious laws and all the precepts of the Sabbath.

Paula ends with a kind of theology of immortality in the form of a vision or mystical revelation:

> I felt myself sinking into that cool water, and knew that the voyage through pain was ending in an absolute void. As I dissolved, I had the revelation that the void was filled with everything the universe holds. Nothing and everything, at once. Sacramental light and unfathomable darkness. I am the void, I am everything that exists, I am in every leaf of the forest, in every drop of dew, in every particle of ash carried by the stream, I am Paula and I am also Isabel, I am nothing and all other things in this life and other lives, immortal.
>
> Godspeed, Paula, woman. Welcome, Paula, spirit.[13]

In a completely secular manner, outside institutional religion and without even a mystical framework, Allende's insights are similar to those of Hedwig of Antwerp, whose intuitions about the void and God linked the experience of the past and the present with men and women who are in search of the source of life and meaning.[14]

God in the Fabric and Weaving of Life

Now we need to develop a feminist perspective on the experience of God in accord with the positions taken in the course of this reflection. More precisely, we are going to enter into a feminist theological analysis using the concept of gender. The feminism aspect is marked by an effort toward a theological deconstruction so that egalitarian relations can be established. While perhaps appearing radical, it is respectful of popular religious expression. This reflection not only has a theoretical significance but also reflects a praxis that is beginning to be developed in various groups of women in Latin America. Here I want to develop two points: God and gender, and the esse-diversity of God.

God and Gender

How do feminists say "God"? How do they express their cry or their sigh toward God, especially in suffering or some evil situation? How do they articulate their appeal to God in view of their criticism of a male God, as he has always appeared in our culture? Is there a feminist theological methodology particular to women's experience?

We approach the experience of God starting with the category of gender. We must stress that this approach lies within the realm of theologizing and is therefore a secondary act in relation to the experience itself of the mystery of God, especially true in the midst of suffering. The first act is the experience itself of suffering in hells of every sort, an experience that hinders at the time any organized thought about God. In the suffering common to every human being is only the cry or sigh begging for relief. There is only an emptiness into which no concept, no explanation can enter. In these extreme situations, reason seems to give way to feelings of pain, anguish, and the grip of suffering. Reason is itself threatened by the irrationality of the evil, by the harshness and the incomprehension of the moment. Reason is wounded by the impossibility of reacting in a sane way in the face of the evil causing the pain. Only an inner cry resists what is threatening us; we pray that the evil be stopped so that God, if possible, will "remove this cup from me" (Mark 14:36). Here we are at the point of immediate experience, at the level of daily suffering, and not at the point of reflecting on the experience.

Reflection about what has happened is at a second level, an interpretive level, full of hypotheses and different solutions so as to try to understand and even change the situation. One tries to analyze what has taken place. One interprets the situation from a certain distance, even if one is still suffering. One tries to understand and explain. One enters into the hermeneutic circle in which different approaches and attempts to understand are possible. This is the point at which we are locating our reflection.

To speak of God and gender is to make two affirmations: first, it is to note that what we say of God is tied to our life experience and that our very idea of God, as well as our relationship with him (her) or that mystery, is determined by what we have described in chapter 2 as a social and cultural construct of gender. More precisely, this means that all our ideas, including our idea of God, are distinguished by the cultural and social dynamics of gender. Like certain feminist theories, I use the concept of gender to show that human sexuality is stamped by the reality of social and cultural influences. The result is an interconnection among men and women's sociocultural relationships, the establishment of social identity, and images or models of God. The concept of God, especially in the Christian tradition, is forged from an understanding of social roles and of justice and transcendence. Feminist theology aims to deconstruct the patriarchal concept of God and thus develop a new understanding of these issues.

If we consider the history of the concept of God and some developments in Christian theology, we can easily observe that not only is this concept primarily male, but also the way God acts, with a few exceptions, is a masculine way of acting in history. He is the creator, the savior, the one who opens doors for his people, the one who satisfies them, leads them, fights on their behalf, protects them, and loves them. Rarely do theologians or other writers depict attitudes of God related to the way women behave in various cultures, even though one may, for example, find such acts in the Bible. God always has great battles to undertake for freedom. He has so many people to save! He is always working, even though the Bible says he rested on the seventh day. He is a serious God, ever busy at keeping order in the universe. Male theologians attempt to show God's concern for the human being, and the concrete manifestation of this concern is always shown in male universalist terms.

Theologians have made an initial stake on a single idea of God, a model of divine goodness, and they often mount a defense of God on this model, which is often opposed to the human individual and serves to accuse the human of infidelity, deviation, or disobedience. We have in this portrayal a universal and idealized understanding of God, based on men's experience, which has become problematic for feminists.[15] Everything is so momentous and so well thought out by God that we always have the impression of living in the order established by God himself. Official theological treatises rarely mention the concrete circumstances of every day—the domestic scene; fragile relationships; violence of every kind; the contradictions of existence, failures, and little joys, as well as the limits of our religious certitudes.

Theology often uses parables and stories of daily life present in the Gospels to justify a cosmo-vision, an interpretation, a moral position, a dogma, a law. It is enough to see, for instance, how biblical commentaries on the parables often try to validate a male point of view, even when they make a positive contribution to social justice.[16] I think this is true also for feminist theologians: they try to take hold of the least clue that can support their position. But what seems foremost in male theological discourse is the general affirmation of the indisputable love of God, his trinitarian character, the communion of the divine persons, the basic goodness of the biblical God. This is an a priori view of God that must always be asserted. Daily experience is not invoked except to confirm what is from all eternity or a priori.

Male theology shows up, then, as a global discourse, with its own language of certitudes claiming to be scientific, even if, here and there, it may speak of suffering or life's limits. We know that even a treatise about certainties is built on the weaknesses of concrete existence and, in one way, tries to go beyond them, to forget them, to give them the least importance in order to assert its own truthful character. Feminism criticizes this approach because it contradicts daily life, particularly that lived by women in various situations and regions of the world. This critique is being developed at the risk of falling itself into other forms of generalization. Therefore we must admit that, even if women theologians want to transcend what they oppose, they run the risk of falling into a revenge with no exit. It is almost inevitable for them not to be influenced by the feeling of always having been considered "the second sex." Still, we have to accept this experience in our history. Along the same lines, we can observe that in our culture all the forms of God's action are spontaneously considered male, even those that might be considered female. The masculine side of God engulfs the feminine, coopts it, makes it his. This is not a value judgment, but a statement—first about the cultural order, then about the theological order. Indeed, the theological is necessarily cultural.

To illustrate, I will take examples from the liberation theology of Latin America. In citing theologians I have no intention of criticizing them personally. In no way am I calling into question their commitment and the seriousness of their work and their struggle for justice in following Jesus. Quite the contrary: they continue to be, for the Christian community of Latin America, important references as teachers and witnesses. What is in question is a structure of thought, an organization of the meaning of life from a cosmo-vision and anthropology that have a limited logic and value today. Still, it is in emerging from this logic that an "other" logic attempts to assert itself, another logic that wants women to be entirely the creators of their own life and of societal life. As André Wénin says so well of Sarai, Abram's wife, it is a question of "coming out of her dependence and existing one day as a subject."[17]

At first glance one might think that the feminist struggle against these theologies belongs to the theoretical order, but I would disagree. If there is a theoretical struggle, it concerns the practical, the understanding of life and of contemporary things happening in neighborhoods and in the organizations of the church. It concerns the education of children and teenagers in the faith. It is a matter of building egalitarian relationships. It is a question of a more contextual way of living the gospel values outside the formalism of faith bound by metaphysics or the formalism of theology full of a priori statements.

The theoretical aspect is the fact that feminism, by criticizing the patriarchal structures of thought, is trying to introduce others. The heart of the question, if there is one, is in the practical order, however. In other words, feminist theology is trying to recover the essential core of the Christian experience, beginning with a different understanding of the relationships between men and women and of humanity's relationship with the whole of creation, by taking seriously people's concrete experience. Similarly, certain feminist theories, which I too endorse, want to relocate religious experience in a meaning under construction day by day, in continuity with our ancestors and along the many paths of tenderness and mercy. In view of this, some examples will help us discern more clearly the problematic proposed and its critique.

In his book *O Deus dos Cristãos* (The God of Christians) the Chilean theologian Ronaldo Muñoz says:

> Justice *(sedaq)* is not a static trait of the divine essence, but a dynamic trait of the character of Yahweh which shows in his action. It is the rectitude of Yahweh's action that "makes" justice. . . .

> The justice of Yahweh appears at once marked by an absolute and sovereign character. Yahweh is in himself the norm of his action. Every ethical standard has its value in reference to the actions of Yahweh, who, for his part, does not let himself be measured by any norm of human invention.[18]

Indeed, there is some truth in these statements, but they deal with an almost idealistic approach to the transcendence of God. We have here a discourse constructed on God or, more precisely, on a model of God with a philosophical referent. The author appears to formulate his statements on the action of God in an almost absolute manner. He reproduces, in an actualized form, the philosophical concept of the prime mover of Aristotle, adapted later in a Christian context by St. Thomas Aquinas. In his turn Muñoz takes up this concept, but from an ethical point of view: it is an ethic tied to a metaphysic. God is the norm of our action, but he says that this God "has no norm of action conceived by humans." What is the experiential basis for these statements? How can they be maintained as a basis for the experience of the human being without reference to the human being?

Feminist theology is trying to open a breach in this discourse and to show that even the justice in the Bible attributed to Yahweh was, at the same time, injustice with regard to other peoples and often to women. For feminist theologians, the transcendence of God does not lie in the fact that someone proves rationally that the action of God is good. This analysis means nothing in face of the web of violence and injustice in which we live. It is not necessary to prove the paternity or the maternity or the goodness of God. One must accept that God is God, that is, that the mystery is mystery, that meaning is meaning beyond the prison of our speech.[19] By adopting this perspective, feminist theology works with more modesty, with more distance than rational patriarchal discourse, as if we were speaking of something we do not really know. It adopts a certain existential silence, even if speech makes itself heard when crossing the threshold of interpretations and publications.

In a contribution to the collective work published in *Mysterium Liberationis*, Leonardo Boff writes:

> The Father is invisible because he is a profound mystery. Jesus reveals it to us clearly: No one has seen God. The only Son who is in the bosom of the Father makes us know him (John 1:18; 1 Tim. 6:16; 1 John 4:12). And he has revealed him exactly as a Father who has a Son and who lives eternally with the Holy Spirit. The intimacy of Jesus with his Father is so great that he has been able to say: "Whoever sees me sees the Father" (John 14:9). The Father is the One who is eternal, even when no other creature existed. He is Father, not because he has created, but because he has engendered the Son and the Holy Spirit. In the Son he has sent forth daughters and sons created and able to create. Thus the Father is the source of all paternity and also of all brotherhood and sisterhood.[20]

Leonardo Boff does not say explicitly that God, invisible mystery, is male, but the language, culture, and theology lead effectively to this understanding. These three factors are part of a game of organizing meaning, and this game obeys certain foreordained rules. In this sense, to do theology is to know how to play the game, to know its rules even if they are far removed from daily life. In practice, even by introducing into the discourse concern for brothers and sisters, the universalist organization of the discourse favors a conception of the world where the male predominates and reduces daily experience, the unspeakable mystery that weaves and constitutes us, to a formal construct called "scientific." This kind of discourse leads to hierarchies and inequalities, especially since what is said to be common to mortals becomes inaccessible. Male theologians may say that this is part of abstraction, proper and necessary for all science. While there is always a level of abstraction in human thought and language, when the abstraction becomes an ideology that promotes the dominance of the knowledge of some over others, this abstraction is no longer knowledge but the politics of domination.

I do not think Leonardo Boff and other theologians intended this result, but no one escapes the traps of the power to know, especially when this power shows itself as a discourse on God, on his design, his holiness, and his mystery. This is how theological discourse can become a discourse of power, threatening and dangerous, because it makes appeal in the last instance to the being of God and his will. And in this realm, simple folk always have the worst of it in arguing or pursuing an open dialogue.

In *O rosto materno de Deus* (The maternal face of God) Leonardo Boff tries to recover the feminine within a structure dominated by the masculine. He wants to find hints of the feminine and to give them value within the masculine. But once again, it is an attempt to salvage inside the same system, and in my view it does not succeed in setting forth the feminine in an egalitarian manner. He writes, "Through the hypostatic union, the humanity of Jesus (masculine and feminine) must be considered the humanity of God. The masculine receives in this way its ultimate divine reference. The feminine is implicit because it forms a part of the human reality of the man Jesus."[21] The feminine is implicit, that is, included in the universalist male discourse: what is included does not appear clearly, is not evident in its own originality. It is an inclusion in something that already has its specific worth. Thus, in spite of his openness and his efforts toward justice among persons, Boff does not succeed in hiding the priority of the male or in establishing the equal dignity of the female. We must note that when feminism refers to inclusive language, the term refers to language in which female and male are explicit, as in *human person* or *men and women* or *brothers and sisters,* instead of simply *man* or *brother*.

These examples from liberation theology do not claim to be a critical analysis of the works cited. Their goal is to illustrate the problematic under consideration and to show the originality of the critique that feminists address to theology. Just as all cultures have left women out of important historical decisions, artistic creation, and literary production, in Christianity women have not been able to express publicly their experience of God. They have received the image of God set before them or taught to them by men or by the dominant culture. This does not mean that they have not re-created these images in the course of their life and context, but this re-creation has stayed in the "little" world inhabited by women. These experiences have not been considered as any contribution to the teaching of the church.

Today we are beginning to discover more and more women who are mystics, saints, religious, or simply mothers of families or celibates who have expressed in some original way their experience of God.[22] Even if this experience is often influenced by male teaching, it is a rich and varied one. But it remains marginal and has never been cited or gained recognition in the church.[23] Often, too, in their religious experience these women identified their sufferings with the sufferings of Jesus. Though that helped them survive, this identification also contributed to maintaining silence about the particular suffering of women, whether at home or in the cloister. As Julia Kristeva says, "The loving identification with the Christ was no doubt the core of this singular adventure that led a woman to undergo the deepest suffering at the peak of serenity: masculine suffering (that of Christ) in which many wounds and feminine humiliations were transferred so as to raise oneself to a glorious self-image."[24] In fact, women's experiences do not enter into religious culture in general, especially not in Latin America.

Theologians and churches have only in small part recovered the spiritual history of women, even those in the Bible. This fact may seem neither important nor interesting. But it is an important factor as we develop an understanding of what it means to introduce the category of gender into the concept of God. With that lens, we note how strictly patriarchal[25] theology has limited the concept of God to a male point of view, even while believing that it is achieving a more universal vision, one that takes in all humanity. Moreover, this theology speaks of God in the name of the church and identifies the teaching of the church with the masculine Magisterium pure and simple. This sort of universalist male pretension, which has excluded different experiences and even often made them impossible, is being rightly denounced by a gender-based analysis. We have here a hermeneutical concept that opens us to a different theological understanding and demands a different way of doing theology.

The image of God conveyed by Christian culture has certainly been multiform. But historically it has invoked a plurality of male images that threw into the shadow every feminine inkling of the Mystery. God the Father, God the Creator, God the Savior, God King of the Universe, God the Judge, God the Son: these images come in great part from Jewish monotheism, deemed an advance over the idolatry of neighboring peoples.[26] A gender-based analysis invites us to introduce other theories of interpretation of certain biblical texts. We begin to suspect that these "other" peoples, with their different cultures, were not so bad after all and that women, reduced in part to a symbol of evil, are not so wicked. These theories come from feminist research in history and biblical exegesis, but also from archaeology and history of religions.[27] The importance of these hypotheses and interpretations resides in the fact that they allow the possibility of thinking otherwise about "the history of God" or "the models of God" that have appeared in the Christian history of various cultures.[28] This research permits recovering the history of women and the feminine faces of God that have not been able to be expressed freely throughout the history of theology.[29]

In this perspective, certain feminists put the accent on the fact that all theology is, somehow, a theopolitic; that is, as theological thought is organized, God sides with certain groups, persons, or situations, and in the last analysis the image of God is fashioned according to our interests. As mentioned earlier, the patriarchal theological world has often assigned to women a secondary place relative to men: it has considered them more impure and more removed from the masculine holiness of God. But that is not simply a biocultural fact: it thrusts its roots into the conflicts of power that follow one another in the course of history and is inscribed in the complex fabric of events, ideologies, and conceptions of life that war among themselves.

In the light of this interpretive key, we read the book of Genesis, for example, as a book that reflects conflicts between political powers. Like all the others, these interpretations are marked by a bias. From a patriarchal perspective, the victory of Yahweh is the victory of the one true God over the idols of barbarians. The struggle among different peoples represents in a way the "struggle among gods." As Monica Sjoo and Barbara Mor write, "The settled people of the Old Testament, like everyone else in the Near East, practiced Goddess worship. The Old Testament is the record of the conquest and massacre of these Neolithic people by the nomadic Hebrews, followers of a Sky God, who then set up their biblical God in the place of the ancient Goddess."[30] Astarte, the female divinity of the Canaanites, represented by the serpent, the tree, or a woman, is confronted by the power of Yahweh, the male God. Yahweh goes with his people into the land of the Canaanites, the promised land, and finds there other deities and another culture.[31] In the biblical texts the confrontation is not clear; what is said and not said must be read between the lines, and other historic sources must also be consulted.

We learn from this confrontation why certain symbols, linked especially to women's experience, become icons of evil. The meaning of symbols sacred to the Canaanites is reversed in order to identify them with evil and to introduce masculine Israelite symbols, such as those that represent the justice and faithfulness of Yahweh. This situation makes me think of the conquest of the Americas, when local deities were replaced or transformed into Catholic symbols. And the first Christian historians described the destruction of peoples as a conquest undertaken in the name of the true belief in God. Destroying the altars of indigenous peoples meant the defeat of a tribe. When a people, for whatever reason, lost belief in its cultural values or was obliged to give them up by force, it lost its identity. In the sixteenth century the Americas experienced this gradual loss of identity. The altars of the goddess

Tonantzin, goddess of the earth, were replaced by altars dedicated to the Virgin Mary. It was partly for this reason that a rapprochement occurred between Tonantzin and the Virgin, not only in the history of the Mexican people but in the cultural customs still operating today.[32] As this procedure was common to all cultures, we should be able to acknowledge, in spite of the sacred character we attribute to biblical history, this identical behavior between the conquerors and the conquered in the case of the Israelite people.

From the same point of view of rereading Genesis, some feminist exegetes raise the question of the sin of Cain, known as the first fratricide, the symbol also of the sin of our origins. Through a careful investigation one can see that Cain was the favorite of his mother, the favorite of the mother of the living. Cain was a farmer, bound to the earth. Abel was a shepherd, a completely male occupation, according to anthropologists, and he was the favorite of Yahweh. A fight broke out between the two. The bad one, the mother's favorite, kills the son of the father. Up to the present day the curse, as we know, is on Cain.[33] Here a power struggle on different levels, subtly brought out by the biblical text, shows the complexity of relationships and behaviors. This is not a question of making Cain less guilty or the crime more acceptable but of seeing that there is a game of strength at play here between masculine/feminine, God/Goddess, son loved by the Mother/son loved by the Father. A gender-based analysis reveals the intricacy of the social and political construct, especially when we are dealing with religious and political forces.

It is interesting to note that the law of the Father (Yahweh) has been transgressed several times and quite particularly by partisans of female structures of power. Eve is not afraid of the serpent; she speaks to it as if it were a familiar. And it is the law of the Father that is "violated." Likewise, in the case of Cain and Abel, this murder is seen as an act against the Father.[34] Nevertheless, the strength of the Father has been historically victorious, even if the powers of dispute are laid bare. The curse falls on the power of Eve, the mother of the living, and has affected her daughters especially. In this perspective Mary, the mother of Jesus, far from representing the victory of female forces, will represent the coopting of female forces by male ones. She "will crush the head of the serpent," the serpent elsewhere said to be the symbol of the Goddess. Since patriarchal culture has retained traces of more feminine cultures, we can see that they have the strength and capacity to bloom again today.[35]

In terms of the Christian experience, it is not hard to see that the basic construct of the Christian message as well as of Christian theologies has been formed on patriarchal models. What is called the privileged revelation of God could be realized culturally only in the form of a man, Jesus. For critical feminist theology the problem is not the fact that Jesus is a man, a part of his own historic identity, but that this man continues even today to be proclaimed the Only Son of God, Savior, and God himself. In other words, culture has insisted on the male character of salvation, even if other approaches could be developed, approaches also contained in our tradition. These approaches could lead to the rise of a theological construct more egalitarian and balanced. As Elisabeth Schüssler Fiorenza has shown so well,[36] I think particularly of the tradition of Wisdom, which, in spite of its limited use in the past, seems to open today a path to more just human relations. In Proverbs we read:

> I, wisdom, live with prudence,
> and I attain knowledge and discretion. . . .
> I walk in the way of righteousness,
> along the paths of justice,
> endowing with wealth those who love me
> and filling their treasuries. (8:12, 20-21)

While aware that the Christian tradition of Wisdom identifies Jesus with Divine Wisdom or the Wisdom of the Logos, can we not suggest that Wisdom be affirmed as one expression of the unfathomable mystery of God? Jesus, prophet of Wisdom, is sent with the mission to heal the hearts of the poor, of the marginalized, of all those who suffer injustice. By placing certain treasures of our tradition in a new light, we may try, on the one hand, to do justice to the mystery of God, which is beyond maternal and paternal images, and, on the other, to do justice to women often excluded from divine symbolism. Taking note of this tradition, we can open new avenues and affirm Jesus as the prophet of Wisdom.[37] He experienced this Wisdom in a special way and was recognized by his disciples, men and women, as a man who walked the paths of justice and righteousness. Wisdom excludes no one. Men and women alike can become her children, her prophets and prophetesses.

Speaking of Wisdom opens a christological reference more inclusive, in the feminist meaning of the term, than that of God, the Father of Jesus. We are not meaning to deny the presence of the Father as a biblical image, but we need to be attentive to the problems raised by the reality of our history. Being attentive will take us into a more flexible hermeneutical perspective. It will allow us to adopt symbolism that is more able to sustain dialogue between different religions and better able to promote justice between men and women. Correlatively this hermeneutic seems to set in relief the responsibility of Jesus' disciples, men and women, in the struggle to keep the good news alive and lived in a community of equals.[38] From this perspective, I am not suggesting that we repudiate the christological formulations of the great Councils but instead that we enlarge theological reflection by raising new challenges proposed by cultural movements. We must situate the formulations in the place where they should remain and broaden the criteria for belonging to a community that claims the tradition of Jesus. The criterion to be recognized as a disciple of Jesus has always been sharing bread, giving help to those who live on the streets, recognizing the dignity of the poor and marginalized. The testimony of Jesus as "coming from God" is, first of all, a testimony to life, a testimony that makes a qualitative difference in human relationship.

Analyzing the ties between evil and a problematic Christology goes beyond the limits of this reflection. Still, I would like to add that this issue plays a prominent part in the discussions and meetings of feminist theologians of Latin America.[39] Similarly, it often comes up in women's groups when they are studying the Bible and trying to discover traces of a tradition that is more egalitarian and respectful of women.

The Esse-Diversity of God

The feminist theology I espouse certainly does not involve either getting rid of male images of God or a radical change in which the oppressed become the oppressors. This not only is impossible but in no way moves human relations toward justice. We are not concerned with an iconoclastic attitude generating violence but with a critical reflection bolstered by new analytical references. Analyses using gender as well as the contributions of contemporary science have given us enough indication about the impossibility of maintaining traditional theological discourse unchanged.[40] Traditional discourse has been, like other knowledge, directly or indirectly complicit in the planetary destruction we are witnessing today.

I believe the first step in this direction is to dare to think of human relations as attempting to overcome the discriminatory and unjust hierarchical connections of our societies and our churches. This would be a common ethical horizon from which we could try again to establish new relations with different groups. This is old hat, no doubt, but now it is extended in a new way in a different historic world context. Today's context is marked by different oppressions intersecting and crossing over one another to form a violent stage on which we live. There are no spaces of innocence, even though responsibilities are not always the same. Our world is surely marked by unjust relations at the level of the social construct of gender, but also in race, nation, and social class. Oppressions become just as complex as the different forces of liberation. Issues seem to be growing more difficult and complicated.

From a theological point of view, we are invited to live and to comprehend the mystery of God every time a new challenge presents itself. From this perspective, Jürgen Moltmann says that ecology demands a new way of thinking about God: "The centre of this thinking is no longer the distinction between God and the world. The centre is the recognition of the presence of God *in* the world and the presence of the world *in* God."[41] Feminist theologians say the same thing and build their thought starting from this fundamental affirmation.

This situation leads us to look for a plural discourse on God or on this mystery that crosses our lives. This is why I propose the expression *esse-diversity of God*. It is certainly not an expression much in use among theologians and will probably raise questions, especially in regard to pantheism or to a possible reductionism of theological language to that of the ecological sciences. In spite of these risks, I think the expression can be used as a new metaphor to express this ever-present reality, one that human beings have always had trouble expressing.

To speak of the esse-diversity of God means to speak first of all of life in its extraordinary richness, but a life that unfolds in the complexity of a vital mystery. This mystery is not outside us, but we are in it and there we exist and evolve. Likewise, this mystery lives in us and beyond us. A good number of the texts of the New Testament, notably the Acts of the Apostles and writings of St. Paul, echo this idea. The concept of esse-diversity favors equally the contribution of all beings, situates them outside hierarchical boundaries, and still does not accentuate any presumed superiority of some over others. I have no illusion about the ability of feminist theology or different models of God to claim that ultimately they have found, with a certain idea or behavior, the path to justice. But faith calls us to free ourselves from every form of oppression that we cause in our history and to look for ways to promote justice and tenderness, equality and friendship. We may not avoid mistakes in the search, but we must always dare to have creativity.

The esse-diversity of God is a metaphor based on the relatedness of everything with everything else: all things live in God and God lives in everything. In this sense, God is that reality that penetrates, crosses, and vivifies every other reality, beyond any good or evil named and carried out by human beings. The awareness of God's esse-diversity drives us to other ways of expressing this relational mystery. Concretely, we will no longer speak of any will or any project as being of God, but rather of human projects to sustain life, valuable for that reason alone.

The esse-diversity of God invites us to a different silence about God, to give up chatter that does not change the heart of life. The esse-diversity of God brings us beyond the anthropological and the androcentric, but it includes them too. Basically, to think about God outside the limitations different theologies have imposed on God is in some way to return to the simplicity of ordinary life. It is to affirm our admiration and silence in a radical way before this relational reality, which is not necessarily a person as we are, not all-powerful, not more perfect, but a mystery that is in all beings. This will invite us to take up the way of Jesus more as an ethic in favor of the life of all than as a metaphysic where a trinity of deities with male faces talk to each other in an exchange of perfections. This approach invites us to move beyond the philosophical refinements customary in theology to find again the experiences of the life of Jesus and our own experiences as places where love takes flesh.

The esse-diversity of God allows us to develop other discourses on the meaning of life, that is, different theologies and a difference of approaches to salvation. If, from early times, to speak of the Christ is linked to Jesus of Nazareth, that does not mean that we cannot open this discourse to many other Christic possibilities in the Christian community. To speak of Christian communities means being constantly open to new possibilities of salvation in which each person and each community will become salvation for the other. We are trying to emerge from the centrality of certain personages, an undue importance that concentrates all responsibility on them, in order that all may share responsibility for the future and in order that all may share the struggle for the salvation of all.

In this way, there will exist a salvation proper to women, in one context and in precise situations, and a salvation proper to men—a salvation demanded by different cultures and a salvation demanded by the ecosystem in its plurality and all its complexity. And, in this salvation with many faces, individuals, women and men, have the special responsibility to be concerned with the suffering and the salvation of one and all. It is certain that this is not the last word on the subject.

These ancient affirmations of our tradition are reawakened, urged by the problematic of our day and by the desire to struggle for life in abundance. This is no question of judging theological statements as true or false, but to ask which one is the best way to present the Christian faith in today's pluralistic context. In other words, we need to think how these different theological approaches can enter into dialogue so as to contribute to the increase of justice for all. Finally, we must not forget that a good part of our theological efforts amounts to nothing other than making clear in many ways, by poetry and metaphor, by discourses and stories, by dreams and desires the unfathomable reality of the "I am who I am" (Exod. 3:14).

epilogue

Now that I have come to the end of this work, the words of Phoolan Devi help me review my reflective journey and express my hope for a feminist approach to the problem of evil.

> All my life I have asked God the same questions: Was I born to suffer? Did I come into the world to be a slave? God of the world, why wasn't I born an animal?
>
> Animals live in freedom and respect in our Hindu society. Even the dog wandering around in search of food has not lived my lot.
>
> If God had made me a man, I would not have had to face this dreadful destiny. It is because I am a woman that I have been humiliated to the depths of my soul.[1]

The last testimony is that of Phoolan Devi, a woman with bloody scars, once queen of bandits and later a deputy of the Indian Parliament.[2] Her testimony brings to mind the reason for this work: the silent oppression endured by so many women, especially those of Latin America. Many women, especially the poorest, are so despised that they ultimately despise themselves as human beings. In light of their lives, we must re-theologize and re-philosophize the problem of evil and salvation. We need to think about their difficulties and their rescue that they may eventually become grateful for being female, rather than wishing that they had been born male. And last, we need to denounce the anti-feminism present in our societies and churches, especially that anti-feminism masked as a democratic overture of benevolence toward all human beings.

Often religious institutions have a preestablished idea of good and salvation, as if these are already known in advance— a universalist idea formulated from a male point of reference. Women have only to adapt themselves quietly to what has already been decided long ago. They have only to conform to ideas divorced from the reality of actual men and women living in concrete situations and various cultures. Such an anti-feminism, so present in the church, conceals our own fear and especially the fear of those in power, fear of thinking and living differently from our present way. This anti-feminism hides fear of the human condition, which invites us always to revisit our convictions, to understand ourselves anew, and to respect one another despite our differences. Against the violence of cultural and religious dogmatism, we must open spaces to hear different voices—voices that disturb, alienate, and irritate but voices that can stir up the waters of our lives and arouse new movements with new hopes and challenges.

One of the goals of this work has been to make known from anthropology and theology the sufferings and humiliations of women, their great and small griefs, so well expressed by Phoolan Devi and many other women. Various witnesses have, one after another, revealed the diversity of evil, its pluriform nature that cannot be reduced to some single theoretical concept. These women have made known in practice not only the existential anguish that informs the lives of human beings, but the anguish of being a woman, that is, a human being considered inferior in comparison to male excellence.

This anthropological and cultural concept, present in different traditions, is in great part responsible for an experience of evil peculiar to women, even though men endure similar experiences of suffering. In this diversity a form of evil has appeared not yet sufficiently recognized by Christian theology. It is the evil undergone and experienced especially by women at home and within social structures, like the church, that were originally founded to love and help people find dignity. We have provided an opportunity not only to listen to this evil but also to think about it, using interpretive means common to feminism. This evil in our being, inherited from our mothers, our culture, and Christianity, has been set in relief, so to speak. This book has set out to unveil this evil so as to enable us to have a dialogue about daily behaviors that have become habits, which are intermingled with injustices.

The phenomenology of evil as women see it has attempted to show a pluriform evil experienced on the domestic scene, present in places where women dwell, occurring because of their status as women. These evils, embedded in families, homes, brothels, convents, churches, and theologies, have become public and are now objects of scientific research. In other words, these evils are entering the academic world, the world of scientific knowledge, hitherto the world of men. Women are beginning to be able to speak, to emerge from their silence, to share their pains and gain a certain public recognition. Naming the evils women endure opens a breach in the universalizing discourses of our theologies. This naming means taking up the experiences that are near at hand, taking tears, pains, sufferings, and little joys as matters for reflection. We are forced to consider in daily life short-term relations and disappointments in love, death, and mourning as experiences capable of balancing the coldness of figures, statistics, and theological positions that follow preestablished rules. Women's stories, literary writings, poetry, theology, or merely cries of distress or joy in life, give new substance to theological research.

The concept of gender, a new, primarily feminist hermeneutical tool, has allowed us to emerge, on the one hand, from a dualistic vision of being human and, on the other, from a certain anthropological naïveté that considers male humanity as normative for all. Gender has allowed us to see how the male–female relationship is based on a hierarchical vision and male superiority, and how gender itself is a cultural, social, and political construct capable of fostering and heightening evil. Indeed, the concept of gender has revealed the perception of the world and the human being as playing power games in the social roles attributed to men and women. There are social consequences in this power game for both men and women.

There is a social pride in being a man. It becomes a sort of passion, called *machismo* in Latin America, and it causes a certain crassness before others' troubles, using them as a disposable consumer item. In contrast, women have a lack of self-esteem on the personal and collective levels, resulting in a certain passivity and causing them to accept their inferior role like an inescapable destiny. The contradictions considered in this work have revealed further hidden digressions on human evil. Gender has become a tool that has led not only to a better understanding of the cultural situation of men and women but also to setting up a system to gain respect for differences and likenesses.

Thinking about the bad experiences of women leads to thinking about ways they too commit evil. We have noted that victims are not virtuous or morally good just because they are victims. A complicity in evil includes victims as well as oppressors and holds them responsible for satisfying our penchant to destroy others. Thus, from accusations against the patriarchal system comes an understanding of everyone's personal responsibility in evil, even though the level of responsibility is not always the same. The anthropological notion of "mixture," though not specially dealt with, has hovered over the whole of this work. We human beings are always this mixture of greatness and pettiness, of good and evil, of hot and cold. We are this mixture that allows us to identify ourselves, as Paul Ricoeur would say, in our limitedness and infinity, in our dimensions of voluntary and involuntary, in our desire for love and for hate. The notion of mixture has allowed us the possibility of revisiting Christian ideas on human evil and our origins and has invited us to analyze them from new reference points.

Finally, as Phoolan Devi says in the foreword of her book, women's testimonies have shown their uneasiness about God: they have shared their cries to the mysterious being to whom we address our lamentations and sighs. What is the face of God for women, particularly for those women cited in this book? This question has taken up the last chapter of our thought and shown us the richness of experience in the chiaroscuro of daily life. At the end of this work we can ask: What changes do these thoughts about evil and new concepts bring to a theology that wants to be liberating?

First, introducing feminism into theology and using gender in hermeneutics demand a more inclusive and contextual anthropology. Phenomenology has given us concrete stories of women in their despair and hope. This has meant taking our history—yesterday's and today's—seriously. Theologically speaking, we are invited to believe in the power of the Spirit that creates (not just preserves) tradition. This point of view leads us to modify our patriarchal reading of the Bible and allows us to introduce other perspectives and points of reference. We are today more attuned to different groups who open the Bible to dialogue, who look there for an exchange of insights in putting together what has been and is still being experienced today.

I have spoken of the human being as a rich mixture of what we call good and evil, and in this way, I have tried to go beyond our tradition that says that first there was good, then evil came on the scene, and after this there will be again the complete reign of good. We have insisted on this category of mixture in order to show what was and what is human. The evolution of life, which leads us to the fascinating appearance of the human, seems to situate us in this mixture, even if some myths about origins give us other explanations.

We claim from our daily experience that individuals or groups of men and women of splendid human quality have not yet brought about a process of growth in virtue over the years in such a way as to make the human substance of today better than it was earlier. In this constitutive human mixture we need to look for love and justice and solidarity. For this reason we have spoken insistently about the crosses and, at the same time, the paths of resurrection, the paths of concrete salvation. Similarly, we have spoken of the cross of Jesus, while trying to give more importance to his acts of redemption, mercy, justice, and friendship than to the cross imposed by an imperial power as the symbol of his life. These saving acts give us life and ought to be the major symbols of our faith. To this end, the idea of relatedness appears to us as a concept capable of helping us understand what it means to be human beings, more inclusive and interdependent than other beings. This notion makes us emerge from hierarchical models that have characterized our anthropology and our theology and opens us to a perspective more circular and embracing of all beings.

Then we spoke of God for women, a God with many faces and yet faceless. This is a God mingled with the daily routine of poor women who cry to him/her in the midst of their struggle simply to survive; a baroque God sometimes clement and sometimes stern, present in cloisters and libraries, inspiring love poems and love for poems; a God critical of his own images, images frozen in a patriarchal world, likened to an army, to emperors and kings, to philosophical systems and theological treatises; a God who cries within us to be free from our prisons, who cries to be allowed to be simply God, the One who *is*. From the phenomenology of evil, we have arrived at silence on the mystery that dwells in us and in whom we dwell, Mystery in all and beyond all. This path allows us to accept the changes proposed in our theological discourse in the heart of the life of various Christian communities and in fidelity to the tears, dreams, and hopes of people.

In the end I appeal to Phoolan Devi and ask her to lend me her words to bring my reflection to a close.

> This book is the first one written by a woman of my community. It is a hand extended to the poor and humble with the hope that a life like mine will never be repeated.
>
> I would like it to help me kill ignorance, stamp out scorn and domination. May it give courage to my sisters, women, and to my brothers, the wretched, the exploited.
>
> I want to say loud and strong that we all have honor, whatever our origin, our caste, the color of our skin, or our sex.

I want respect. I want it for myself and for all human beings.[3]

Phoolan Devi, that is what I want too.

notes

Introduction

1. For a different approach to evil beginning with tradition and leading to a new anthropology, see Adolph Gesché, *Dieu pour penser,* vol. 1, *Le Mal* (Paris: Cerf, 1993).

2. See Augustine of Hippo, *De Trinitate,* 7,7,10, cited by Rosemary Radford Ruether, *Sexism and God-Talk: Toward a Feminist Theology* (Boston: Beacon, 1983), 95. See also Jean-Marie Aubert, *L'exil féminin: Antiféminisme et Christianisme* (Recherches morales 11; Paris: Cerf, 1988), and Augustine, *De Trinitate,* 12,7,9–12, in *Oeuvres de St. Augustin,* trans. Paul Agaësse (Bibliothèque Augustinienne, vol. 16; Paris: Desclée de Brower, 1955), 228–35 (text and French translation).

3. This problem will be treated in detail in chapter 5.

4. Jean-Claude Guillebaud, *The Tyranny of Pleasure,* trans. Keith Torjoc (New York: Algora, 1999). See also Régine Pernoud, *Women in the Days of the Cathedrals,* trans. and adapt. Anne Côté-Harriss (San Francisco: Ignatius, 1998).

5. Jean Delumeau, *La Peur en Occident* (Paris: Hachette, 1999).

6. Aubert, *L'exil féminin,* 179.

7. For a critical overview of feminist theology in North America and Europe, see Hedwig Meyer-Wilmes, *Rebellion on the Borders,* trans. Irene Smith-Bouman (Kampen, Netherlands: Ed. Kok Pharos, 1995).

8. Ibid., 52.

9. Andrée Michel, *Le Féminisme* (Que sais-je?; Paris: Presses universitaires de France, 1979; rep. 1997). See also "Femme," in *Encyclopaedia Universalis* (Paris: Encyclopaedia universalis France, 1968), 6:973–1010.

10. This term is used not only by feminists, but also by historians and an ethicist, such as Aubert, *L'exil féminin*, 5.

11. See Nicole Claude Mathieu, "Identité sexuelle/sexuée/de sexe: Trois modes de conceptualisation du rapport entre sexe et genre" in idem, *L'anatomie politique: Catégorisations et idéologies du sexe* (Paris: Côté-Femmes, 1991); idem, "Études feministes et anthropologiques," in *Le Dictionnaire de l'Ethnologie et de l'Anthropologie*, ed. Pierre Bonte, Michel Izard, and Marion Abélès (Paris: Presses universitaires de France, 1992); Jeanne Bissiliat, *Relations de genre et développement: femmes et sociétés*, ed. Florence Pinton and Mireille Lecarme (Collection Colloques et séminaires; Paris: l'ORSTOM, 1992); and *Qu'est-ce que le féminisme?* (Montréal: CEDEAC et Relais Femmes, 1997).

12. Bila Sorj, "O feminismo na encruzilhada da Modernidade e Pos-Modernidade," in Albertina de Oliveira Costa and Cristina Bruschini, eds., *Uma Questão de Gênero* (Rio de Janeiro/São Paulo: Ed. Rosa dos Tempos/Fundação Carlos Chagas, 1992), 25.

13. On this subject see Jean-François Lyotard, *Phenomenology*, trans. Brian Beakley (SUNY Series in Contemporary Continental Philosophy; Albany: State University of New York Press, 1991).

14. Paul Ricoeur, *Philosophy of the Will*, trans. Charles Kelbley (Chicago: Regnery, 1965).

Chapter 1: Women's Experience of Evil

1. Edmund Husserl, *Idées directrices pour une phénoménologie*, trans. Paul Ricoeur (Paris: Gallimard, 1950). See also Jean-François Lyotard, *Phenomenology*, trans. Brian Beakley (SUNY Series in Contemporary Continental Philosophy; Albany: State University of New York Press, 1991).

2. Hannah Arendt, *Eichmann in Jerusalem: A Report on the Banality of Evil* (rev. and enl. ed.; New York: Penguin, 1965), 298.

3. This perspective is developed in several works. Besides the texts used in this chapter, see Jean-Paul Sartre, *The Words,* trans. Bernard Frechtman (New York: Vintage, 1981); Simone de Beauvoir, *Memoirs of a Dutiful Daughter,* trans. James Kirkup (Cleveland: World, 1959); and Simone Weil, *La condition ouvrière* (Paris: Gallimard, 1964).

4. Kamala Markandaya, *Nectar in a Sieve* (New York: Day, 1955).

5. Ibid., 111.

6. Ibid., 124.

7. Ibid., 250–52.

8. Ibid., 136.

9. On this subject see Paul Ricoeur, *Oneself as Another,* trans. Kathleen Blamey (Chicago: University of Chicago Press, 1992).

10. Frances O'Gorman and mulheres da Rocinha e de Santa Marta, *Morro, Mulher* (Coleção O Povo quer viver 11; São Paulo: Paulinas, FASE-Programa NUCLAR, 1984), 13.

11. Carolina Maria de Jesus, *Child of the Dark: The Diary of Carolina Maria de Jesus,* trans. David St. Clair (New York: Dutton, 1962).

12. Ibid., 146, 152, 29, 153.

13. Isabel Allende, *Paula,* trans. Margaret Sayers Peden (New York: HarperCollins, 1995). Isabel Allende has just published a book on the pleasure of eating and the awakening of the senses, *Aphrodite: A Memoir of the Senses,* trans. Margaret Sayers Peden (New York: HarperFlamingo, 1998).

14. Allende, *Paula,* 3.

15. Ibid., 9–10.

16. Ibid., 205.

17. Ibid., 271.

18. Ibid., 325.

19. This idea will be discussed in chapter 5, "God for Women."

20. Violeta Parra, *Décimas: Autobiographía en verso* (Santiago, Chile: Sudamericana, 1988).

21. Ibid., 117.

22. Ibid., 145.

23. Juana Inés de la Cruz, "Respuesta de la poetisa a la muy ilustre Sor Filotea de la Cruz," in *Obras Completas* (Mexico City: Porrúa, 1989), 830.

24. Juana Inés de la Cruz, "Redondillas," in *Poesía Lírica,* ed. José Carlos Gonzales Boixo (Madrid: Cátedra Letras Hispánicas, 1992), 222.

25. Octavio Paz, *Soeur Juana Inés de la Cruz ou les pièges de la foi* (Paris: Gallimard, 1987).

26. See the response Juana Inés wrote to the bishop who accused her of deviating from her religious life, "Respuesta," in *Obras Completas.*

27. *Yo, la peor de todas*: an extraordinary film by the Argentinean filmmaker Maria Luisa Bemberg. According to information supplied by Octavio Paz (*Soeur Juana,* 114), the formula *Yo, la peor de todas* (I, the worst of all), appears under the poet's signature and also on a page of the book of professions at the convent of St. Jerome.

28. Paz in *Soeur Juana* gives numerous references on the work of various interpreters of Sister Juana Inés. There are a number of words dedicated to the life and thought of Sister Juana Inés, including, for example, Stephanie Merrim, "Toward a Feminist Reading of Sor Juana Inés de la Cruz," in idem, ed., *Feminist Perspectives on Sor Juana Inés de la Cruz* (Detroit: Wayne State University Press, 1991).

29. Paz, *Soeur Juana,* 111.

30. Ibid.

31. Gilberto Dimenstein, *Meninas da noite: A prostituição de meninas-escravas no Brasil* (2d ed.; São Paulo: Atica, 1992), 25.

32. Ibid., 47.

33. Ibid., 26.

34. Lenira, *Só a gente que vive que sabe: Depoimento de uma doméstica* (Cadernos de Educação Popular 4; Petrópolis: Vozes/Nova, 1984), 17.

35. Ibid., 18.

36. Delores S. Williams, *Sisters in the Wilderness: The Challenge of Womanist God-Talk* (Maryknoll, N.Y.: Orbis, 1993), 85.

37. The word *mulatto* brings to mind *mules,* animals that can carry heavy burdens and serve their masters without complaint.

38. Toni Morrison, *The Bluest Eye* (New York: Plume, 1994).

39. Williams, *Sisters in the Wilderness,* 88.

40. Alice Walker, *The Color Purple* (New York: Pocket Books, 1982), 1.

41. Ibid., 6.

42. My understanding of matriarchs, mothers of families in the Orient who bear a very important role in the culture, is a Western-ized understanding and limited to a context of cultural "transplan-tation." On the subject of matriarchs see the interesting work of Catherine Chalier with a preface by Emmanuel Levinas, *Les Matriarches: Sarah, Rebecca, Rachel et Léa* (Paris: Cerf, 1985).

43. Gustavo Gutiérrez, *A Theology of Liberation: History, Politics, and Salvation,* trans. and ed. Sister Caridad Inda and John Eagle-son (Maryknoll, N.Y.: Orbis, 1973), 15.

44. See Kari Elisabeth Børresen, *Subordination and Equivalence: The Nature and Role of Women in Augustine and Thomas Aquinas,* trans. Charles H. Talbot (Washington, D.C.: University Press of America, 1981). See also Rosemary Radford Ruether, *Sexism and God-Talk: Toward a Feminist Theology* (Boston: Beacon, 1989).

45. See, for example, Elisabeth Schüssler Fiorenza, *Discipleship of Equals: A Critical Feminist Ekklesia-Logy of Liberation* (New York: Crossroad, 1993), and Rita Nakashima Brock, *Journeys by Heart: A Christology of Erotic Power* (New York: Crossroad, 1994).

46. Gutiérrez, *Theology of Liberation,* 145.

47. Paul Ricoeur, *Philosophy of the Will,* trans. Charles Kelbley (Chicago: Regnery, 1965).

Chapter 2: Evil and Gender

1. Theories about gender developed toward the end of the twen-tieth century. They can be found in numerous works published by French-speaking feminists, but especially by white feminists in North America. Examples include the works of the Belgian philosopher Françoise Collin, such as "Praxis de la différence:

Notes sur le tragique du sujet," in *Cahiers de GRIF,* no. 46 (1992). See also Julia Kristeva, *Tales of Love,* trans. Leon S. Roudiez (New York: Columbia University Press, 1987), and Luce Irigaray, *This Sex Which Is Not One,* trans. Catherine Porter with Carolyn Burke (Ithaca, N.Y.: Cornell University Press, 1985). Other works of French authors are cited in the introduction to this work. On the North American side, see Joan Scott, "Gender: A Useful Category of Historical Analyses," in *Gender and the Politics of History* (New York: Columbia University Press, 1989), 28–50, 206–11.

2. On this subject see Kari Elisabeth Børresen and Kari Vogt, *Women's Studies of the Christian and Islamic Traditions: Ancient, Medieval, and Renaissance Foremothers* (Dordrecht, Netherlands: Kluwer Academic Publishers, 1993).

3. See Julia Kristeva, "Le temps des femmes," *Cahiers de recherches en sciences des textes et documents* (1979), n. 5, and Scott, "Gender." Scott, a sociologist, shows how strongly the category of gender can decode the meaning of certain human relations and interactions between them. Moreover, she deals with the way gender legitimates different mores in different cultures.

4. Françoise Heritier, *Masculin/Féminin: La pensée de la différence* (Paris: Odile Jacob, 1996).

5. See the interesting treatment by Elisabeth Schüssler Fiorenza in her book *But She Said: Feminist Practices of Biblical Interpretation* (Boston: Beacon, 1992).

6. Interview with Erilda in *Mouvement pour l'Habitation,* Capão Redondo, São Paulo (July 14, 1994). Photostat text in the archives of the Movement.

7. See, for example, Kathleen Sands, *Escape from Paradise: Evil and Tragedy in Feminist Theology* (Minneapolis: Fortress Press, 1994); Elaine Pagels, *Adam, Eve, and the Serpent* (New York: Vintage, 1989); and Emilie M. Townes, ed., *A Troubling in My Soul: Womanist Perspectives on Evil and Suffering* (Maryknoll, N.Y.: Orbis, 1993).

8. My main reference here is Scott, "Gender."

9. Elisabeth Badinter, *The Unopposite Sex: The End of the Gender Battle,* trans. Barbara Wright (New York: Harper & Row, 1989).

10. Pierre Bourdieu, "A dominação masculina," *Revista Educação e Realidade*, São Paulo (July/December 1995), 133–34, and idem, "Novas reflexões sobre a dominação masculina," in *Gênero e Saúde*, ed. Marta J. Lopez, Dagmar Meyer, Vera Waldow (Pôrto Alegre: Artes Médicas, 1996). See also Pierre Bourdieu, *The Logic of Practice*, trans. Richard Nice (Stanford, Calif.: Stanford University Press, 1990).

11. Luce Irigaray, *Thinking the Difference: For a Peaceful Revolution*, trans. Karin Montin (New York: Routledge, 1994).

12. Catharine MacKinnon, "Feminism, Marxism, Method, and State: An Agenda for Theory," in *Feminist Theory: A Critique of Ideology*, ed. Nannerl O. Keohane, Michelle Z. Rosaldo, and Barbara C. Gelpi (Chicago: University of Chicago Press, 1982), 1–30.

13. Seyla Benhabib, *Situating the Self: Gender, Community, and Post-Modernism in Contemporary Ethics* (New York: Routledge, 1992).

14. Phyllis Trible, *Texts of Terror: Literary-Feminist Readings of Biblical Narratives* (Overtures to Biblical Theology; Philadelphia: Fortress Press, 1984).

15. Michelle Perrot, *Une histoire des femmes est-elle possible?* (Paris: Rivage, 1984).

16. Kari Elisabeth Børresen, *Subordination and Equivalence: The Nature and Role of Woman in Augustine and Thomas Aquinas*, trans. Charles H. Talbot (Washington, D.C.: University Press of America, 1981).

17. The same perspective is developed in the catechism of the Catholic church.

18. See Emmanuel Levinas, *Existence and Existents*, trans. Alphonso Lingis (Pittsburgh, Pa.: Duquesne University Press, 2001), and *Humanisme de l'autre homme* (Paris: Le Livre de Poche, Biblio Essais, 1972).

19. Paul Veyne, ed., *From Pagan Rome to Byzantium*, vol. 1 of *A History of Private Life*, ed. Philippe Ariès and Georges Duby (Cambridge, Mass.: Belknap Press of Harvard University Press, 1987).

20. René Girard, *The Scapegoat*, trans. Yvonne Freccero (Baltimore: Johns Hopkins University Press, 1986), 21.

21. René Girard, *Violence and the Sacred*, trans. Patrick Gregory (Baltimore: Johns Hopkins University Press, 1977), 146.

22. Mary Daly, *Beyond God the Father: Toward a Philosophy of Women's Liberation* (Boston: Beacon, 1973), 75–77.

23. See, for example, Joanne Carlson Brown and Carole R. Bohn, eds., *Christianity, Patriarchy and Abuse: A Feminist Critique* (Cleveland, Ohio: Pilgrim, 1989).

24. Rigoberta Menchú, *I, Rigoberta Menchú: An Indian Woman in Guatemala*, ed. Elisabeth Burgos-Debray, trans. Ann Wright (London: Verso, 1984), esp. ch. 10.

25. See Carolyn Merchant, *The Death of Nature: Women, Ecology and Scientific Revolution* (New York: Harper & Row, 1989); also Maria Mies, Veronika Bennholdt-Thomsen, and Claudia von Werlhof, *Women: The Last Colony* (London: Zed, 1988).

26. On this subject see H. Kramer and J. Spranger, *O Martelo das feiticeiras (Malleus Maleficarum)* (6th ed.; Rio de Janeiro: Rosa dos Tempos, 1991)—documents that describe the punishments the Inquisition imposed on a number of women thought to be possessed by the devil.

27. John Paul II, *Mulieris dignitatem* (The dignity and vocation to motherhood) (São Paulo: Paulinas, 1988).

28. See Leonardo Boff, *The Maternal Face of God: The Feminine and Its Religious Expressions*, trans. Robert R. Barr and John W. Diercksmeier (San Francisco: Harper & Row, 1987), and Luis Perez Aguirre, *La condición femenina* (Montevideo, Uruguay: Trilce, 1995)—an interesting avant-garde work of a Uruguayan theologian.

29. See "Spirituality for Life: Women Struggling against Violence," in VOICES, *Ecumenical Association of Third World Theologians*, New Delhi, June 1994; "Women's Experience of the Sacred," ibid., June 1996.

30. Paul Ricoeur, *Philosophy of the Will*, trans. Charles Kelbley (Chicago: Regnery, 1965), and *The Symbolism of Evil*, trans. Emerson Buchanan (New York: Harper & Row, 1967).

31. Paul Ricoeur, "Culpabilité tragique et Culpabilité biblique," *Revue d'Histoire et de philosophie religieuses* (Paris, 1953).

Chapter 3: The Evil Women Do

1. Zygmunt Bauman, *Postmodern Ethics* (Oxford: Blackwell, 1993), 227, 228.

2. Laura Esquivel, *Like Water for Chocolate: A Novel in Monthly Installments, with Recipes, Romances, and Home Remedies*, trans. Carol Christensen and Thomas Christensen (New York: Doubleday, 1992).

3. Ibid., 10.

4. Carolyn Merchant, *The Death of Nature: Women, Ecology and Scientific Revolution* (San Francisco: Harper & Row, 1989). See also Maria Mies and Vandana Shiva, *Ecofeminism* (London: Zed, 1993).

5. See the work of the French psychoanalyst Christiane Olivier, especially *Jocasta's Children: The Imprint of the Mother*, trans. George Craig (London and New York: Routledge, 1989). The explanation she gives of the psychological and social role of the mother presents a different understanding from the Oedipus complex.

6. Margareth Rago, *Os prazeres da noite: Prostituição e códigos de sexualidade feminina em São Paulo, 1890–1930* (Rio de Janeiro: Paz e Terra, 1991).

7. Ibid., 245.

8. Ángeles Mastretta, *Arráncame la vida* (Buenos Aires: Alfaguara, 1996).

9. See, for example, the article of Rita Nakashima Brock, "And a Little Child Will Lead Us: Christology and Child Abuse," in Joanne Carlson Brown and Carole R. Bohn, eds., *Christianity, Patriarchy and Abuse: A Feminist Critique* (Cleveland, Ohio: Pilgrim, 1989).

10. Dorothee Soelle, "Fatherhood, Power, and Barbarism," in *The Window of Vulnerability* (Minneapolis: Fortress Press, 1990).

11. See Alice Dermience, "La question de Dieu et la représentation de Dieu: Un défi pour la théologie féministe," *E/T Bulletin de l'Association Européenne de Théologie Catholique*, 1994/1, 40–50, esp. 43–47.

12. On this topic see Joanne Carlson Brown and Rebecca Parker, "For God So Loved the World?" in Brown and Bohn, eds., *Christianity, Patriarchy and Abuse*.

Chapter 4: Women's Experience of Salvation

1. Several psalms reflect this mixture in life. For example:

> May those who sow in tears
>   reap with shouts of joy.
> Those who go out weeping,
>   bearing the seed for sowing,
> shall come home with shouts of joy,
>   carrying their sheaves. (Ps. 126:5-6)

2. The cross, for Christians a symbol bound to the life of Jesus, is also a universal symbol, like the circle or the dot. On this subject see Gérard de Champeaux and Dom Sébastien Sterckx, O.S.B., *Introduction au monde des symboles* (2d ed.; Saint-Léger-Vauban [Yonne]: Zodiaque, 1972).

3. Ibid., 365–73.

4. Workshop, "Para além da violência," Praia do Janga, Paulista, PE, from September 25 to 28, 1997.

5. J. B. Libânio, "Sinodo dos bispos para a América: Entre o Pessimismo e a Esperança, in Tempo e Presença, Rio de Janeiro," *Set/Out* 1997.

6. See Elisabeth Lacelle, "Oser la Réconciliation," in *Femmes et Hommes en Église*, Bulletin International, n. 69, Paris, March 1997, 25–27.

7. See René Girard, *The Scapegoat,* trans. Yvonne Freccero (Baltimore: Johns Hopkins University Press, 1986).

8. See Jürgen Moltmann, *The Crucified God: The Cross of Christ as the Foundation and Criticism of Christian Theology,* trans. R. A. Wilson and John Bowden (Minneapolis: Fortress Press, 1993).

9. See Adolphe Gesché, *Dieu pour penser,* vol. 4, *Le Cosmos* (Paris: Cerf, 1994).

10. Adolphe Gesché, *Dieu pour penser,* vol. 5, *La Destinée* (Paris: Cerf, 1995), esp. 105–12.

11. Cf. Julia Kristeva, "Le bonheur des béguines," in *Le jardin clos de l'âme: L'imaginaire des religieuses dans les Pays-Bas du Sud depuis le 13e siècle,* Société des expositions, Palais des Beaux-Arts de Bruxelles, February 25–May 22, 1994.

12. Ivone Gebara, "Pour une spiritualité au quotidien," trans. Paul Tihon, in *La Foi et le Temps,* Tournai, 1994, vol. 4, 355–66.

13. On Jesus and the poor, see Jon Sobrino, *Christology at the Crossroads: A Latin American Approach,* trans. John Drury (Maryknoll, N.Y.: Orbis, 1978). See also the remarkable work of Joseph Moingt, *L'homme qui venait de Dieu* (Cogitatio fidei 176; Paris: Cerf, 1994).

14. Jung Mo Sung, *Deus numa economia sem coração: Pobreza e neoliberalismo* (São Paulo: Paulinas, 1992).

15. Brian Swimme, "Science: A Partner in Creating the Vision," in Anne Lonergan and Caroline Richards, eds., *Thomas Berry and the New Cosmology* (Mystic, Conn.: Twenty-Third Publications, 1987), 87, cited in Sallie McFague, *The Body of God: An Ecological Theology* (Minneapolis: Fortress Press, 1993), 106.

16. The book by Ilya Prigogine and Isabelle Stengers, *Order Out of Chaos: Man's New Dialogue with Nature* (Boulder, Colo.: New Science Library and Random House, 1984), helps us think in this direction.

17. Robert M. Augros and George N. Stanciu, *The New Story of Science: Mind and the Universe* (Lake Bluff, Ill.: Regnery Gateway, 1985). See also Ilya Prigogine, *Les lois du Chaos* (coll. Champs 369; Paris: Flammarion, 1994).

18. Adolphe Gesché, *Dieu pour penser,* vol. 1, *Le Mal* (Paris: Cerf, 1993).

19. Paul Ricoeur, *Fallible Man,* trans. Charles Kelbley (Chicago: Regnery, 1965), 3.

20. Rubem Alves, *A Festa de Maria* (São Paulo: Papirus, Campinas, 1997), 24.

Chapter 5: God for Women

1. M. Guerrin, "Une madone en enfer," *Le Monde* (September 26, 1997), 12.

2. Even though this is a feminist work, I use the male pronoun for God because this is how poor women think of God.

3. Several important works have been published on popular culture in Latin America, among which is the classic by Oscar Lewis, *The Children of Sanchez: Autobiography of a Mexican Family* (New York: Random House, 1979).

4. Octavio Paz, *Soeur Juana Inés de la Cruz ou les pièges de la foi* (Paris: Gallimard, 1987), 454. "The Dream" is a poem written by Sister Juana Inés in 1690.

5. Juana Inés de la Cruz, "Respuesta de la poetisa a la muy ilustre Sor Filotea de la Cruz," in *Obras Completas* (Mexico City: Porrúa, 1989), 845.

6. Paz, *Soeur Juana,* 78.

7. Juana Inés de la Cruz was accused by the Inquisition of having a "particular friendship" with the vice-queen, her protector.

8. De la Cruz, *Obras Completas,* 167.

9. De la Cruz, "Dos Letras sueltas para cantar en la solemnidad del nacimiento," in *Obras Completas,* 316.

10. De la Cruz, "Letras Sagradas en la Solemnidad de la profesión de una religiosa," in *Obras Completas,* 318.

11. De la Cruz, "Letra III – De las Antifonas," in *Obras Completas,* 319.

12. Melano Beatriz Couch, "Soror Juana Inés de la Cruz: The First Woman Theologian in the Americas," in John C. B. Webster and Ellen Low, eds., *The Church and Women in the Third World* (Louisville, Ky.: Westminster John Knox, 1985).

13. Isabel Allende, *Paula,* trans. Margaret Sayers Peden (New York: HarperCollins, 1995), 330.

14. "Greetings! First source in ourselves, who gives us noble heavenly knowledge and the food of love, ever renewed, and who preserves us in your wisdom from every mishap coming from outside. The unity of the naked truth, doing away with all reason, holds me in this emptiness," Hadewijch d'Anvers [Hedwig of Antwerp], *Écrits mystiques des Béguines* (Points Sagesses, 65; Paris: Seuil, 1954), 211.

15. See Alice Dermience, "La question de Dieu et la représentation de Dieu: Un défi pour la théologie féministe," *E/T Bulletin de*

l'Association Européenne de Théologie Catholique, 1994/1, 40–50, esp. 40–41.

16. See Jacques Dupont, *Pourquoi des paraboles? La méthode parabolique de Jésus* (Lire la Bible, 46; Paris: Cerf, 1977), and especially *Les Béatitudes II et III* (2d ed.; Études bibliques; Paris: Gabalda, 1973).

17. André Wénin, *Abram, fils de Tèrakh: Une interprétation de Genèse*, 11, 26-32, in E.E.S.P.R. (20, 1996), 147.

18. Ronaldo Muñoz, *O Deus dos Cristãos* (Petrópolis: Vozes, 1986), 169.

19. We must again recall that feminism is a pluralistic cultural phenomenon. To say "Feminism says this or that" really implies "Certain forms of feminism, and particularly the one I endorse." The temptation to universalize is always present.

20. Leonardo Boff, "Trinidad, Conceptos Fundamentales de la Teología de la Liberación," in Ignacio Ellacuría and Jon Sobrino, eds., *Mysterium Liberationis: Conceptos fundamentales de la teología de la liberación* (Madrid: Trotta, 1990), 526–27.

21. Leonardo Boff, *O rosto materno de Deus* (Petrópolis: Vozes, 1979), 10.

22. Régine Pernoud, *Hildegard of Bingen: Inspired Conscience of the Twelfth Century*, trans. Paul Duggan (New York: Marlowe, 1998); and Hadewijch d'Anvers, *Écrits mystiques des Béguines*.

23. For example, the delicate and spirited work of Marguerite Porete, fruit of the spirituality of the thirteenth century, is rarely mentioned in Catholic theological circles. See Marguerite Porete, *Mirror of Simple Souls*, trans. Ellen L. Babinsky (New York: Paulist, 1993).

24. Julia Kristeva, "Le bonheur des béguines," in *Le jardin clos de l'âme: L'imaginaire des religieuses dans les Pays-Bas du Sud depuis le 13e siècle* (exhibit catalog), Société des expositions, Palais des Beaux-Arts de Bruxelles, February 25–May 22, 1994.

25. Here and elsewhere I use the term *patriarchal* to describe a structure of culture and thought that attributes to man (the male) the privilege of being the main organizer of society. Made up of

Patêr (Father) and Archê (power principle), this word carries the meaning of hierarchical power that permeates social life.

26. Process theology deals with this problem. See Alfred North Whitehead, *Process and Reality* (New York: Free Press, 1978), particularly chapter 2, "God and the World."

27. See the works, for example, of Elisabeth Schüssler Fiorenza, Rosemary Radford Ruether, Daphne Hampson, Carter Heyward, Luise Schottroff, and Monica Sjoo.

28. Sallie McFague, *Models of God: Theology for an Ecological Nuclear Age* (Philadelphia: Fortress Press, 1987).

29. Mary Daly, *Beyond God the Father: Toward a Philosophy of Women's Liberation* (Boston: Beacon, 1973). See also Michel Dion, *Libération féministe et salut chrétien: Mary Daly et Paul Tillich* (Recherches, nouvelle série 29; Montreal: Bellarmin, 1995).

30. Monica Sjoo and Barbara Mor, *The Great Cosmic Mother: Rediscovering the Religion of the Earth* (San Francisco: Harper & Row, 1987), 264.

31. Ibid.

32. Virgilio P. Elizondo, *Guadalupe: Mother of the New Creation* (Maryknoll, N.Y.: Orbis, 1997).

33. Sjoo and Mor, *The Great Cosmic Mother.*

34. This interpretation differs widely from that of André Wénin, *L'homme biblique: Anthropologie et éthique dans le Premier Testament* (Théologies bibliques; Paris: Cerf, 1995).

35. Susan Niditch, *Genesis,* in Carol Newsom and Sharon H. Ringe, eds., *The Woman's Bible Commentary* (Louisville, Ky.: Westminster John Knox, 1992).

36. Elisabeth Schüssler Fiorenza, *Jesus—Miriam's Child, Sophia's Prophet: Critical Issues in Feminist Christology* (New York: Continuum, 1994), 139–40.

37. Ibid. See also Denis Edwards, *Jesus, the Wisdom of God: An Ecological Theology* (Maryknoll, N.Y.: Orbis, 1995). The theme of Wisdom here takes on a theological-ecological dimension.

38. See the excellent book of Elizabeth Johnson, *She Who Is: The Mystery of God in Feminist Theological Discourse* (New York: Crossroad, 1993).

39. Number 22 (December 1997) of *Con-Spirando* (a journal published by an ecofeminist group in Santiago, Chile) is completely devoted to answers women gave to the question, "And you, who do you say that I am?"

40. Adolphe Gesché, *Dieu pour penser*, vol. 4, *Le Cosmos* (Paris: Cerf, 1994). See also Thomas Berry and Thomas Clarke, *Befriending the Earth: A Theology of Reconciliation between Humans and the Earth* (Mystic, Conn: Twenty-Third, 1991), and Rosemary Radford Ruether, *Gaia and God: An Ecofeminist Theology of Earth Healing* (San Francisco: Harper, 1992).

41. Jürgen Moltmann, *God in Creation: A New Theology of Creation and the Spirit of God* (Minneapolis: Fortress Press, 1993), 13.

Epilogue

1. Phoolan Devi, *Moi, Phoolan Devi, reine des bandits*, with Marie-Thérèse Cuny (Paris: Fixot, 1996), 7.

2. Phoolan Devi was killed by masked gunmen outside her home on July 2, 2001, at the age of thirty-seven.

3. Phoolan Devi, *Moi*, 8.

a select bibliography

Adams, Carol J., ed. *Ecofeminism and the Sacred.* New York: Continuum, 1993.

Beauvoir, Simone de. *Memoirs of a Dutiful Daughter.* Translated by James Kirkup. Cleveland: World, 1959.

———. *The Second Sex.* Translated and edited by H.M. Parshley. Everyman's Library 137. New York : Knopf, 1993.

Benhabib, Seyla. *Situating the Self: Gender, Community, and Post-Modernism in Contemporary Ethics.* New York: Routledge, 1992.

Børresen, Kari Elisabeth. *Subordination and Equivalence: The Nature and Role of Women in Augustine and Thomas Aquinas.* Translated by Charles H. Talbot. Washington, D.C.: University Press of America, 1981.

Bourdieu, Pierre. *The Logic of Practice.* Translated by Richard Nice. Stanford, Calif.: Stanford University Press, 1990.

———."A dominação masculina." *Revista Educação e Realidade.* July/December 1995.

Brock, Rita Nakashima. *Journeys by Heart: A Christology of Erotic Power.* New York: Crossroad, 1994.

Brown, Joanne Carlson, and Carole R. Bohn, eds. *Christianity, Patriarchy and Abuse: A Feminist Critique.* Cleveland, Ohio: Pilgrim, 1989.

Chopp, Rebecca S. *The Power to Speak: Feminism, Language, God.* New York: Crossroad, 1989.

Chung, Hyun Kyung. *Struggle to Be the Sun Again: Introducing Asian Women's Theology*. Maryknoll, N.Y.: Orbis, 1990.

Daly, Mary. *Beyond God the Father: Toward a Philosophy of Women's Liberation*. Boston: Beacon, 1973.

Esquivel, Laura. *Like Water for Chocolate: A Novel in Monthly Installments, with Recipes, Romances, and Home Remedies*. Translated by Carol Christensen and Thomas Christensen. New York: Doubleday, 1992.

Gebara, Ivone, and Maria Clara Bingemer. *Mary: Mother of God, Mother of the Poor*. Translated by Phillip Berryman. Maryknoll, N.Y.: Orbis, 1989.

———. *Teologia ecofeminista*. São Paulo: Ôlho d'Agua, 1997.

Gilligan, Carol. *In a Different Voice: Psychological Theory and Women's Development*. Cambridge, Mass.: Harvard University Press, 1993.

Grant, Jacquelyn. *White Women's Christ and Black Women's Jesus: Feminist Christology and Womanist Response*. American Academy of Religion academy series 64. Atlanta: Scholars, 1989.

Hampson, Daphne. *Theology and Feminism*. Oxford: Blackwell, 1990.

Harding, Sandra. "The Instability of the Analytical Categories of Feminist Theory." *Signs* 11. 1986.

Hunt, Mary. *Fierce Tenderness: A Feminist Theology of Friendship*. New York: Crossroad, 1991.

Irigaray, Luce. *This Sex Which Is Not One*. Translated by Catherine Porter with Carolyn Burke. Ithaca, N.Y.: Cornell University Press, 1985.

Isasi-Díaz, Ada María. *En la Lucha/In the Struggle: Elaborating a Mujerista Theology*. Minneapolis: Fortress Press, 1993.

———. *Mujerista Theology: A Theology for the Twenty-First Century*. Maryknoll, N.Y.: Orbis, 1996.

Johnson, Elizabeth. *She Who Is: The Mystery of God in Feminist Theological Discourse.* New York: Crossroad, 1993.

————. *Women, Earth, and Creator Spirit.* The Madeleva Lecture in Spirituality. New York: Paulist, 1993.

Jones, Serene. *Feminist Theory and Christian Theology: Cartographies of Grace.* Guides to Theological Inquiry. Minneapolis: Fortress Press, 2000.

Kristeva, Julia. "Le temps des femmes." *Cahiers de recherches en sciences des textes et documents.* 1979.

————. "Le bonheur des béguines." In *Le jardin clos de l'âme: L'imaginaire des religieuses dans les Pays-Bas du Sud depuis le 13e siècle.* Société des expositions, Palais des Beaux-Arts de Bruxelles. February 25–May 22, 1994.

MacKinnon, Catharine. "Feminism, Marxism, Method, and State: An Agenda for Theory." In *Feminist Theory: A Critique of Ideology.* Edited by Nannerl O. Keohane, Michelle Z. Rosaldo, and Barbara C. Gelpi. Chicago: University of Chicago Press, 1982. 1–30.

McFague, Sallie. *Models of God: Theology for an Ecological, Nuclear Age.* Philadelphia: Fortress Press, 1987.

————. *The Body of God: An Ecological Theology.* Minneapolis: Fortress Press, 1993.

Merchant, Carolyn. *The Death of Nature: Women, Ecology and Scientific Revolution.* New York: Harper & Row, 1989.

Moltmann-Wendel, Elisabeth. *Rediscovering Friendship: Awakening to the Power and Promise of Women's Friendships.* Minneapolis: Fortress Press, 2001.

Newsom, Carol A., and Sharon H. Ringe, eds. *The Women's Bible Commentary.* Expanded edition. Louisville, Ky.: Westminster John Knox, 1998.

Noddings, Nel. *Women and Evil.* Berkeley: University of California Press, 1989.

Pagels, Elaine. *Adam, Eve, and the Serpent.* New York: Vintage, 1989.

———. *The Origin of Satan.* New York: Random House, 1995.

Ruether, Rosemary Radford. *Sexism and God-Talk: Toward a Feminist Theology.* Boston: Beacon, 1983.

———. *Gaia and God: An Ecofeminist Theology of Earth Healing.* San Francisco: Harper, 1992.

———. *Women and Redemption: A Theological History.* Minneapolis: Fortress Press, 1998.

Russell, Letty M., and J. Shannon Clarkson, eds. *Dictionary of Feminist Theologies.* Louisville, Ky.: Westminster John Knox, 1996.

Sands, Kathleen M. *Escape from Paradise: Evil and Tragedy in Feminist Theology.* Minneapolis: Fortress Press, 1994.

Schneiders, Sandra M. *The Revelatory Text: Interpreting the New Testament as Sacred Scripture.* 2nd ed. Collegeville, Minn.: Liturgical, 1999.

Schüssler Fiorenza, Elisabeth. *In Memory of Her: A Feminist Theological Reconstruction of Christian Origins.* New York: Crossroad, 1983.

———. *But She Said: Feminist Practices of Biblical Interpretation.* Boston: Beacon, 1992.

———. *Jesus—Miriam's Child, Sophia's Prophet: Critical Issues in Feminist Christology.* New York: Continuum, 1994.

———. *Bread Not Stone: The Challenge of Feminist Biblical Interpretation.* Boston: Beacon, 1995.

———. *The Power of Naming: A Concilium Reader in Feminist Liberation Theology.* Maryknoll, N.Y.: Orbis, 1996.

Schüssler Fiorenza, Elisabeth, ed., with the assistance of Shelly Matthews. *Searching the Scriptures.* 2 volumes: *A Feminist Introduction* and *A Feminist Commentary.* New York: Crossroad, 1993–94.

Soelle, Dorothee. *The Silent Cry: Mysticism and Resistance.* Minneapolis: Fortress Press, 2001.

Trible, Phyllis. *Texts of Terror: Literary-Feminist Readings of Biblical Narratives.* Overtures to Biblical Theology. Philadelphia: Fortress Press, 1984.

————. *God and the Rhetoric of Sexuality.* Overtures to Biblical Theology. Philadelphia: Fortress Press, 1986.

Townes, Emilie M., ed. *A Troubling in My Soul: Womanist Perspectives on Evil and Suffering.* Maryknoll, N.Y.: Orbis, 1993.

Williams, Delores S. *Sisters in the Wilderness: The Challenge of Womanist God-Talk.* Maryknoll, N.Y.: Orbis, 1993.

index